Moving Partners from Shattered to Strong

Mending After Betrayal

BOOK AND WORKBOOK

LAURA BURTON

Becoming Well, LLC

Mending After Betrayal

BOOK AND WORKBOOK

Copyright © 2023 by Becoming Well, LLC

All rights reserved. No part of this book may be reproduced or transmitted in any form, or by any means, electronic or mechanical, including photocopying, recording, or by information storage or retrieval systems, without permission in writing from the copyright owner.

The views and opinions expressed in this book are those of the author, and do not necessarily reflect the official policy or position of Becoming Well, LLC

Published by Becoming Well, LLC
www.MyBecomingWell.com
Library of Congress Control Number
Paperback ISBN: 979-8-8690-3383-3
E-book ISBN: 979-8-8690-3398-7

Cover design by Monira

Printed in the United States of America

Table Of Contents

Acknowledgments — ix
Authors note — xi
Introduction — xiii

CHAPTER 1
Types of Infidelity — 1

CHAPTER 2
Recovery Overview — 12

CHAPTER 3
Roadblocks to Healing — 23

CHAPTER 4
Safety in Disclosure — 28

CHAPTER 5
Asking Questions — 39

CHAPTER 6
Meanings, Handling Suspicion, and Polygraph — 50

CHAPTER 7
Boundaries — 58

CHAPTER 8
Self-Care and Self-Compassion — 76

CHAPTER 9
Betrayal and Grief 88

CHAPTER 10
Standard Grief Models 96

CHAPTER 11
An Unconventional Grief Model and Grieving Tips 107

CHAPTER 12
Anger 115

CHAPTER 13
The Destructive Side of Anger 123

CHAPTER 14
Using Anger to Your Advantage 137

CHAPTER 15
Triggers and Reminders 144

CHAPTER 16
Loss of Confidence and Self-Worth 151

CHAPTER 17
Fear 162

CHAPTER 18
Dealing With Fear 168

CHAPTER 19
What is Forgiveness? 179

CHAPTER 20
What Forgiveness Isn't and Practical Steps to Forgiveness 186

CHAPTER 21
Reconciliation 198

CHAPTER 22
Letting Go of the Past 207

CHAPTER 23
Life Beyond Betrayal 213

CHAPTER 24
Trusting Yourself Again 218

CHAPTER 25
Post-Traumatic Growth 229

References 234

Acknowledgments

Behind this book stand numerous people who helped, encouraged, and believed in me and in this work. I want to thank my family, friends, fellow recovery coaches and counselors I have worked with along the way. I would also like to thank the members of my Mending After Betrayal women's group. It has been a privilege to work with you and I thank you for giving insight into the content of this book.

I would especially like to thank my mother, Patricia, for her support and love throughout this process. Thank you, Mom. I love you. Also, I would like to give a big shout out to my husband, Matt, with whom I do this work. Thank you for your support and encouragement over the years and for challenging me to keep going.

Authors note

Although the publisher and the author have made every effort to ensure that the information in this book was correct at press time and while this publication is designed to provide accurate information in regard to the subject matter covered, the publisher and the author assume no responsibility for errors, inaccuracies, omissions, or any other inconsistencies herein and hereby disclaim any liability to any party for any loss, damage, or disruption caused by errors or omissions, whether such errors or omissions result from negligence, accident, or any other cause.

This publication is meant as a source of valuable information for the reader, however it is not meant as a substitute for direct expert assistance. If such a level of assistance is required, the services of a competent professional should be sought.

Laura Burton

www.MyBecomingWell.com

Introduction

This book is a combination of a book and a workbook. Originally, I had planned to separate the two. However, after looking at it, I decided to incorporate the workbook exercises to prevent the reader from having to flip back and forth between two books. As you read along, you will notice that there are journaling exercises scattered throughout the text. The exercises pertain to the section of reading that precedes them and are designed to help you get more out of what you read by applying it to your specific situation.

The idea for this book/workbook came to me by way of my daily work with individuals and couples attempting to heal their relationships, and themselves, from the devastating effects of infidelity and addiction. Although I love what I do and consider it a privilege to be a part of my client's recovery journeys, I am only one person and, therefore, can't reach as many people as I would like to. By offering the information contained here, I hope to reach many more people than I am able to currently reach. The information and exercises I have included come from my training through the American Association for Sex Addiction Therapy (AASAT), what has worked for me in my own personal recovery, as well as from what my clients share with me about what works for them. If you follow the guidelines I have outlined, I believe you will find what works for you as well.

A little bit about my background. I am a trained and certified Partner's Recovery Coach (PRC), Partner Betrayal Trauma Coach (PBTC), Sexual Recovery Coach (SRC), and Intimacy Anorexia Coach® (IAC) through the American Association for Sexual Addiction Therapy (AASAT). I am also a nationally certified life coach (NCLC) through The Addictions Academy and the co-founder of Becoming Well. At Becoming Well, we specialize in helping individuals and couples heal from the effects of infidelity, sexual addiction, and intimacy avoidance. I have helped hundreds of people just like you find their way back to themselves again after being rocked to the core by these issues.

On a personal note, you should know that I am not a stranger to the devastation of infidelity. My first marriage was to a sexually addicted man who had multiple affairs during the brief time we were married. Although no two experiences are alike, and I don't claim to know exactly what you are going through, I thought it was important for you to know that I have personal experience with the subjects covered here. Unfortunately, my first marriage didn't survive because my husband at the time was unwilling to enter recovery and continued with his infidelity-related behavior. Looking back on it, I wish that I had known that I needed infidelity-specific help in order to heal from what I had experienced. Instead, I did some general counseling and thought that would suffice. It wasn't until my second marriage to Matt, who is the other co-founder of Becoming Well, that I realized how much baggage that I had carried into our relationship. As a result, I have spent years in counseling and engaging in self-help techniques to try to overcome the trauma of my first marriage as well as from my childhood. This is another reason I wanted to write *Mending After Betrayal*. Although I understand that it won't be a magic pill for your recovery, I hope that, by offering these tools, I can help make your recovery time more productive and less lengthy than my own.

Throughout our marriage, Matt and I have struggled to find our way out of the labyrinth that is intimacy avoidance. When I met Matt, I knew that he had struggled in the past with pornography addiction, but I also knew that he had many years of sobriety under his belt and so I felt safe. However, very shortly after we got married, it became apparent that there was something wrong. He was always too busy to spend time with me, was highly critical, blamed me for most of the problems in our marriage, and played the victim when I tried to point out ways in which he was being hurtful to me. It wasn't until we found information on intimacy anorexia® from Dr. Doug Weiss that we realized what was going on. As a partner of an intimacy avoidant husband, I understand the nuances of what this issue brings into relationships. If you want to learn more about the symptoms of intimacy anorexia and intimacy avoidance, please visit our website at https://www.mybecomingwell.com.

I have designed the Mending After Betrayal book and workbook for anyone who has been wounded by the different forms of infidelity that Matt and I work with every day. This includes sexual infidelity, emotional infidelity, infidelity through pornography addiction, and the complicating factor of intimacy avoidance/intimacy anorexia®. Whether you are staying in your relationship and want to try and move forward, feel personally stuck in your recovery, feel traumatized by your partner's infidelity-related behavior, or are not sure whether you want to stay with your partner or not, this material has been designed especially for you. If you are someone who is contemplating leaving your current relationship, I advise that you work thoroughly through the material found in these pages before you make your decision. I think you will find, even if you do end up leaving, that doing the work will help you feel confident that you are making the best decision possible—whatever that decision ends up being.

The road to recovery after infidelity is long and, at times, very difficult. My best advice is that you take it in small chunks and get help where and when you need it. I would also advise that, as you work through the material contained here, you minimize your commitments and non-essential activities in order to take care of yourself during this difficult time in your life. Healing from the effects of infidelity and addiction take a toll on us—body, soul, and spirit. Self-care during this time in your life is essential, and I highly encourage you to put yourself at the top of your priority list. Good nutrition, adequate sleep, and the support of a coach, counselor, and safe friends will all help you stay strong on your journey. In the work that I do, I see people get better every day from the same tools that I have given you here. I know that you can get better as well. I also want to note that the information and suggestions here are meant to guide you toward your healing but are easier understood than practically applied. The fact of the matter is that you have sustained deep injuries, and it will take time and patience to heal those injuries. My best advice to you in to practice self-compassion when it comes to your healing. It's not going to be helpful for you if you shame yourself for not being where you think you "should" be.

Here's to finding the information, hope, and encouragement that you need in order to move forward. And here's to giving yourself the time and patience required to accomplish that.

Best,

Laura

CHAPTER 1

Types of Infidelity

You may have heard the cliché "time heals all wounds"— Not only is it generally unhelpful when people say that to a hurting person, but it is also mostly untrue. Although time can be helpful to the healing process, it's not so much the aspect of time that's important to healing but what a person chooses to do with that time. By reading this book, you have chosen to be productive with your time. Whether staying in your current relationship is feasible or not, it's important that you recognize how crucial it is to give time and attention to your own recovery. The fact that you have decided to dedicate your time to this book and workbook tells me that you are ready to take the first courageous steps towards your own healing and recovery.

Types of Infidelity

When Matt and I work with couples and individuals, we touch on 3 different types of infidelity and one common complicating factor. Although many of the consequences to the wounded partner from the different types of infidelity are the same, there are some unique differences that I would like to highlight here.

Sexual Infidelity

When we think "infidelity", this type is typically what comes to most people's minds. In my work, I use this term to describe infidelity related to physical "cheating". This involves the wounding partner engaging in sexual contact with another person who is not their partner, breaking a vow, promise, or commitment in the act of betrayal. The term "sexual contact" does not only apply to the traditional view of sex. I use the acronym HOVA to include sex of any kind involving hand (H), oral (O), vaginal (V), or anal (A). We want to be clear that any type of HOVA sex is considered cheating. Additionally, I consider any type of fondling or groping, over or under the clothing, to be cheating. The general rule of thumb is that if you would not do it in front of your committed partner, then you are engaging in an act of betrayal.

Sexual infidelity creates intense and long-lasting pain and trauma for the wounded partner. It does something to the partner's spirit, body, and mind that is absolutely devastating. The wounded partner has had their rights and body violated to an extreme degree. When we are in a relationship that is monogamous (or assumed to be), there is an understanding that we are only sharing our body with our partner and our partner is only sharing their body with us. When our partners go outside of that agreement, they not only betray our trust, but they violate us and expose us to harm. They have taken something that is only meant for the two people in the committed relationship and shared it with another person. The result is heartbreaking.

Common reactions of partners who have been wounded by sexual betrayal include:

Rage	Intrusive Thoughts	Flashbacks
Lowered Self-Image	Undereating	Overeating
Emotional Outbursts	Physical Symptoms	Hyperarousal
Sleeplessness	Obsession or Fixation on Obtaining Details	
Spiritual Crisis	Insecurity	Inability to Trust

1. Did this section give you a new perspective on sexual infidelity? If so, what new perspective did you gain?

_____
_____
_____
_____
_____

2. Did you relate to any of the common reactions to sexual betrayal? If so, which ones? List any that you have experienced that aren't listed here.

_____
_____
_____
_____
_____

Emotional Infidelity

I define emotional infidelity as a situation in which a person chooses to share an intimate, emotional connection with someone other than their partner. Emotional infidelity is different than a platonic friendship in that it typically involves some sort of romantic or sexual tension, even if the feelings associated with the tension are never physically acted upon. It is considered a betrayal because it involves a person focusing their emotional energy on someone else that should be going toward their partner. This focus shift creates distance in the relationship and the wounded partner is left to wonder why their partner chose to allow someone else into their emotional world.

The main difference between sexual and emotional infidelity is sexual contact. With sexual infidelity, the parties involved meet face-to-face and have sex (although, sometimes technology such as phones and computers is used). With emotional infidelity, there is often a meeting of the parties involved but the purpose is to connect emotionally without engaging in sex. This is not to say that flirting, innuendos, and even promises aren't often exchanged. I would add here that emotional cheating does not have to involve both parties. I have had clients in my office that have had emotional attachments to other people who did not reciprocate their feelings or even know that the person had feelings for them. This scenario can still cause devastation to the relationship because it is a betrayal of the assumed mutual exclusivity of romantic emotional energy within the relationship. Whether it was reciprocated or not is irrelevant. It is not uncommon for the wounding partner to engage in mental comparisons between the two people, resulting in criticalness toward their partner as well as a general dissatisfaction in the overall relationship. The pain to the wounded partner's heart is profound. Make no mistake, this kind of infidelity feels like betrayal because it is.

People sometimes argue that a deep, emotional attachment to someone other than their partner can't cause remotely the same harm as sexual infidelity, but nothing could be further from the truth. Emotional infidelity can cause the following personal and relational injuries to a wounded partner:

Overeating	Undereating	Sadness
Distance	Confusion	Anger
Lowered Self-Image	Damaged trust	Insecurity
Inability to Trust	Fixation on Finding "The Truth"	

To make matters even more challenging, suspicious partners are frequently gaslit and told that they are crazy for being jealous when their gut is telling them there is something questionable happening. Gaslighting is a form of covert emotional abuse in which a person is intentionally misled by another person who presents a false narrative; leading the person to question their own perception of reality. Gaslighting can take place in all kinds of relationships, with or without infidelity involved. However, it seems to be especially prevalent in relationships where infidelity is occurring, and very heavily present during an emotional affair.

Over time, victims of gaslighting can develop the following problems:

Anxiety	Depression	Feelings of Isolation
Psychological Trauma	Low Self-Esteem	Self-Doubt

1. Have you experienced gaslighting in your relationship in terms of emotional infidelity? If so, how? How has this affected you?

_____
_____
_____
_____
_____

Infidelity Through Pornography

Whether the use of pornography for sexual gratification is infidelity or not is a hotly debated topic. I hold the firm belief that using pornography for sexual gratification is infidelity and, as such, there will be a sense of betrayal and loss associated with this behavior.

Many use the argument that "looking isn't cheating". However, pornography use encompasses much more than simply "looking". The use of pornography for sexual purposes typically involves masturbation and a resulting orgasm. This is problematic not only in the relationship, but for the person using pornography as well. During sex, orgasm, and even afterwards, three extremely powerful, mood-boosting chemicals are released – dopamine, endorphins, and oxytocin. Dopamine plays a major role in reward-motivated behavior. Pornographic scenes are a supranormal stimulus. Viewing these hyper-stimulating images and masturbating to them often leads to unnaturally high levels of dopamine that can't typically be reproduced in a long-term, committed relationship. (Hilton, 2013). As a result, satisfaction in a normal, healthy sexual encounter can be viewed as failing to meet expectations. Additionally, this constant release of powerful chemicals during viewing and, ultimately, orgasm can lead the person to prefer porn usage to sex with their partner.

Studies have shown that those who use pornography on a regular basis tend to struggle in their relationships. Everything from decreased commitment to less sexual satisfaction has turned up in several studies regarding porn usage. (Bridges, et. al., 2003) (Rasmussen, 2016) (Lambert, et. al., 2012). Pornography creates a type of counterfeit intimacy that the user can control. This can lead to unrealistic expectations when it comes to attempting to have a close relationship with an actual human being where intimacy will be expected. When someone is using porn, they are in a fantasy world where there aren't any expectations placed on them personally. The object of their pornographic lust and fantasy is always interested, ready, and able to fulfill all of their sexual desires and curiosities. Their sole purpose is to please them sexually and, when that particular fantasy no longer suits their fancy, another fantasy is just a mouse click away. Most of us know that this simply isn't how the real world works. Unfortunately, regular porn usage can create a mindset in the person who uses it that they are entitled to receive sexual gratification anytime, anywhere, and any way they want it without having to do much, or anything at all, for anyone in return. Pornography users who develop this type of mindset often blame their partners for falling short of their unrealistic expectations.

Another problem with pornography use is the fact that it is typically concealed from the partner. Studies have shown that the number of women that believe their partner does not view porn is significantly higher than male partners who report that they don't view porn. (Carroll, etc. al., 2017) (Zitzman, Butler, 2009). This highlights an obvious disconnect between the two partners. The concealment of porn usage can lead the wounded party to feel that their partner isn't trustworthy because "concealment" really amounts to lying and deception. This is key when considering whether or not porn usage is a form of infidelity. Let us forget for the moment that porn users are expending a significant amount of sexual energy outside of the relationship and note that they are also lying about it in most cases. Lying to our partners is a form of betrayal which can lead to significant problems in our relationships. Trust is the foundation for a healthy, sound relationship. (Lancer, 2018). The mere act of keeping secrets will eventually undermine any relationship. (Iniguez, et. al., 2014). People whose partners view pornography have reported the following negative effects:

Lowered Self-Image	Feelings of Inadequacy	Sexual Pressure
Humiliation from Participation in Certain Sex Acts		Feelings of Betrayal
Feelings of Helplessness	Distrust in Their Partner	Stress
Withdrawal from partner	Despair	Anger

1. Did you learn anything new from this section about infidelity through pornography? If so, what did you learn?

_____
_____
_____
_____

2. Do you personally see pornography as a form of infidelity? Why or why not?

_____
_____
_____
_____

The Complicating Factor of Intimacy Avoidance

This is perhaps the most unique form of betrayal that I work with. Although I believe that it is a type of infidelity because the avoidant person is loyal to themselves instead of their partner, many wounded partners see it as more of a complicating factor. Whether a partner sees this as infidelity or not, all partners I have worked with consider it betrayal. Unlike the other forms of infidelity where the wounding partner is looking for connection outside of their relationship, the intimacy avoidant is trying to avoid connection at all costs.

The term intimacy avoidance refers to a situation in which one partner is avoiding closeness with the other partner in multiple ways. Intimacy avoidance is so automatic that many of the behaviors associated with it go unnoticed by the intimacy avoidant yet can have lasting and devastating effects on their loved ones. This is different from the term Intimacy Anorexia©, coined by Dr. Doug Weiss, who defines it as the *active and intentional* withholding emotionally, sexually, and/or spiritually from a partner for the purpose of creating distance and pain. (Weiss, 2010). The main difference is that the intimacy anorexic knows what they are doing and continues their behavior, and the intimacy avoidant may be unaware of or only partially aware of how they're distancing themselves from their partner. The distance-making behaviors are so ingrained, that most of them are automatic. Another big difference is that Weiss classifies intimacy anorexia® as an addiction. Although some of the behaviors seen in intimacy-avoidant behaviors are similar to those observed in someone who struggles with addiction, we view intimacy avoidance as an operating system as opposed to an addiction. Both conditions most often show up only in the marriage or primary romantic relationship of the intimacy avoidant or intimacy anorexic.

Signs of Intimacy Avoidance and Intimacy Anorexia®

Here are some signs and symptoms to look for:

- Can't seem to commit fully to the relationship

- Often holds the partner to impossible, unattainable standards

- Is perfectionistic and/or feels unlovable when they aren't perfect

- Has a history of short-term relationships, unless the relationships were long-distance

- Stays so busy with work and projects that they have little time to spend with their partner

- Has little to no trust in their partner, even if they've earned it

- When issues/arguments arise, the person's first response is to put the blame back on their partner

- Has little to no empathy

- Plays the victim, especially after being confronted with wrongdoing on their part

- Seems distant during sex or frequently avoids sex

- Acts like listening to their partner's feelings is a huge imposition and/or extremely taxing

- Seems overly sensitive to criticism

- Valid issues are dismissed with a "just get over it" attitude

- Refrains from showing love to their partner in ways they know the partner needs or appreciates

- Refuses to praise or compliment the partner

- Refuses to attend church, pray, or participate in other spiritually focused events with their partner, even though these are normal activities for them

- Is unwilling or unable to share true feelings with their partner

- Uses anger, disapproval, and/or silence as a means to control or punish their partner

- Has ongoing or ungrounded criticism of their partner and verbalizes it, or frequently seems silently angry

- Gets overly angry and/or upset when challenged

- A sexless marriage. Approximately 15% to 20% of couples are in sexless marriages—meaning they do not engage in any sexual activities with their partner or have sex fewer than 6 times per year. Although a sexless marriage does not always signify marital instability or unhappiness, it can be a symptom of living with an intimacy avoidant.

As previously stated, the reason I consider intimacy avoidance to be a type of unfaithfulness is because, as you can see from the list above, the intimacy avoidant (IA) withholds themselves in just about every way imaginable from their partner. I believe this is a form of betrayal, especially when the IA was attentive during the dating phase but pulled away once they got married. Unfortunately, this is often the case – especially when it comes to Intimacy Anorexia®. The unsuspecting spouse of the IA is lured into marriage under false pretenses, and, during the marriage, it is a bait-and-switch scenario. If you had known that you'd be alone in your marriage, you likely wouldn't have signed up for it.

A key area where an IA will avoid intimacy is through withholding sex from their partner. This is a condition known as sexual anorexia. The term "withholding sex" can mean the actual withholding of sex, but it can also mean that the IA is disconnected emotionally during sex. I have also seen situations in which IAs will have sex with their partners but will pick fights before or after and/or stress their partners out with an unrealistic set of expectations around sex to ensure that the sex they have with their partner is disconnected. This can be done intentionally or unintentionally, but it is always done because the intimacy avoidant is uncomfortable with any type of intimate connection that might happen during sex.

I would like to mention here that we rarely see intimacy avoidance in our office without at least some accompanying porn usage. I believe the reason for this is that pornography and intimacy avoidance complement each other. Pornography and masturbation allow the IA to have their sexual needs met without any risk of connection to their partner. Although porn usage is the most common, we see other forms of infidelity in combination with IA as well. For the IA, everything is about driving enough distance between themselves and the partner that they no longer feel uncomfortable. If your partner is an IA, it's important that they deal with this aspect of their behavior because it typically drives other infidelity-related behavior.

The effects on partners of IAs can vary. However, here are some common ones that I see in my office:

Depression	Anxiety	Confusion
"Muddied" Thinking	Feelings of Helplessness	Low Self-Esteem
Overeating	High Levels of Anger	
Withdrawal from Friends and Family		

Many of these effects happen because gaslighting is frequently a feature of IA relationships. (Gaslighting is a form of emotional abuse where the person doing the gaslighting is trying to get a person or group of people to question their own memories or perceptions of reality.) For example, it is not uncommon for an IA (especially an intimacy anorexic®) to say things like, "I never said that" even though their partner knows that they did say it.

Additional examples of gaslighting include doing something and then saying they never did it, giving the silent treatment but saying that they are not, saying things like, "I'm sorry that you *think* I hurt your feelings" (implying that they really didn't hurt your feelings), and saying that a situation is your fault because you should have known how they would react. Gaslighting is typically intentional.

1. Do you think you or your partner might deal with intimacy avoidance and/or intimacy anorexia (IA)? Why or why not?

___

2. If you suspect your partner to be IA, how has this affected you and your relationship?

___

CHAPTER 2

Recovery Overview

"To heal, you have to get to the root of the wound and kiss it all the way up."
-Rupi Kaur-

Probably the most common question I get from wounded partners in early recovery is, "Why should I have to do recovery?" This question makes sense, considering the fact that someone else's bad actions are what put us in this place to begin with. If they broke it, they should have to fix it, right? Unfortunately, that idea is wrong. No one has the power to fix someone else, although they can do things that aid or hinder healing. Betrayal is trauma and, once we have been traumatized, the effects of that trauma now reside inside of us. As unfair as it is, it's now our responsibility to deal with the aftermath so that it doesn't affect the rest of our lives.

According to the American Psychiatric Association, the effects of trauma can include increased arousal states, avoidant coping strategies, and flashbacks and/or intrusive thoughts. (APA, 2023). Additionally, research suggests that trauma can create attentional bias as well as negative expectancy bias. (Kimble, et. al., 2018).

Attentional bias is adaptive and is a form of cognitive bias. It's not a bad thing, per se, because it makes it possible for us to pay close attention to things in our environments that may pose danger or threat. (Fisher, 2012).

This allows us to respond quickly to things that have the potential to do us harm. In order to do this, our brain focuses intently on certain things while simultaneously ignoring others in order to make potentially life-saving decisions based on the information given the highest priority. When it comes to unresolved trauma and relationships, this is problematic. Our brains are wired to seek out and pay attention to things that remind us of the trauma. In order to do this, we may be ruling out other information that is pertinent to the decisions we make about our relationships. As one wounded partner told me, "My ex-husband cheated on me and now I see danger everywhere. I can never trust my current partner fully because of this."

Negative expectancy bias is another thing that can come into play where unresolved trauma is concerned. The term describes a situation in which an individual disproportionally expects negative events to happen in both the near and distant future. This can create the need to withdraw or avoid people and unknown situations. As you can see, this has the potential to wreak havoc in relationships because, if a person always expects the negative, they are not likely to want to participate fully or at all in the relationship. The fear of being hurt turns into an expectation of being hurt, causing avoidance of attachment in relationships. While reacting this way can potentially protect us from being hurt in the future, it can also prevent us from making important connections as well as block us from experiencing happiness.

Other ways that unresolved trauma can affect us are as follows:

- Choosing unhealthy relationships and staying in them too long
- Shame-based responses to perceived rejection or criticism
- Unwarranted fight, flight, or freeze responses
- Rigid or negative beliefs about relationships in general
- Chronic stress and hypervigilance

Whether or not a continued relationship with your partner is possible, it is important that you do the work to heal. I like this quote by Richard Rohr that helps explain why:

"The journey to happiness involves finding the courage to go down into ourselves and take responsibility for what's there; all of it."

Or this one, also by Richard Rohr:

"If we do not transform our pain, we will most assuredly transmit it."

The truth is, even though someone else did this to you, it is now a part of your story. As such, we can't pass off the responsibility of healing us to anyone else. We must take responsibility for the pain within ourselves and transform it into something meaningful. If we don't, we run the risk of hurting others – and will most assuredly hurt ourselves – in the process.

1. Does it make sense to you why you need to do your own recovery? Why or why not?

_____
_____
_____
_____
_____

2. What benefits do you think you could gain from doing your own individual recovery?

_____
_____
_____
_____
_____

Personal Recovery vs Relationship Recovery

I would like to talk briefly about the difference between personal recovery and relationship recovery because people seem to get confused between the two. I always say that when couples are trying to recover from infidelity, there are 3 types of recovery going on at once: the recovery for the wounding partner, the recovery for the wounded partner, and the recovery for the relationship.

I lead wounded partners groups every week and I frequently have to clarify this concept. During group check-ins, there's a part of the check-in sheet that says, "I feel _____ about my recovery today." I have noticed a trend where those not getting along with their partners that day or week will report that they feel awful, frustrated, or discouraged about their recovery. I often follow this response up by asking them why they feel that way. More often than not, it is because the relationship isn't going well, or their partner just isn't "getting it". However, when pressed further, they will report that they personally did quite a bit of recovery work that week including workbooks, counseling or coaching, and making phone calls for support. The reason for their initial response had nothing to do with their own personal recovery. It had to do with their partner's recovery or the overall relationship recovery. Do you see the difference?

The truth of the matter is that it is entirely possible for you to recover regardless of whether your relationship or your partner recovers because your personal recovery isn't dependent on the other two. Furthermore, your partner's recovery isn't dependent on your recovery or the recovery of your relationship. Personal recoveries are just that, *personal*. Therefore, each person must take responsibility for their own recovery. No one can do it for them. This simple truth also means that we are not in charge of our partner's recovery. Their recovery is entirely their responsibility.

This does not hold true for the recovery of the relationship. While personal recoveries are independent of each other and of the relationship, the future health of the relationship is completely dependent upon the individual recoveries of the two people involved. When I say, "recovery of the relationship", I am referring to real recovery that allows the trust, intimacy, and safety to return for both parties. It's entirely possible for relationships to technically stay intact without the aid of personal recovery, but they will simply "limp along" and frequently be fraught with tension, anger, and pain. Additionally, it is possible for a relationship to stay together if the wounded partner stays in denial of the problem and excuses the wounding partner's behavior and lack of accountability for that behavior. Neither scenario would qualify (in my opinion) as a healthy, recovered relationship.

1. Do you think you've been confusing your personal recovery, your partner's personal recovery, and your relationship's recovery? Why or why not?

_____
_____
_____
_____
_____

2. Make a list of ways you can tell the difference between the three types of recovery.

_____
_____
_____
_____
_____

The Benefits of Recovery

While I have talked at length about the dangers of not engaging in recovery, I haven't really addressed the wonderful benefits of recovery. The following is a partial list of some of the many benefits of personal recovery:

- Improved sleep
- Improved peace of mind
- Better health
- Ability to smile again
- Positive outlook on life
- Ability to achieve your goals and dreams
- Renewed confidence
- Improved self-compassion and self-acceptance
- Stronger boundaries

- Stronger relationships
- Ability to appreciate and fully enjoy important moments
- Ability to help others in similar situations

1. Out of the above-listed benefits, which ones are the most important to you? Why?

_____
_____
_____
_____
_____

2. Make a list of any additional benefits to personal recovery that come to your mind. Why are these appealing and/or important to you?

_____
_____
_____
_____
_____

Betrayal Trauma

"The saddest thing about betrayal is that it never comes from your enemies."
-Unknown-

Betrayal trauma theory is a concept that was first introduced by Jennifer Freyd, PhD. The term "betrayal trauma" is used to describe a trauma that occurs when a trusted individual, group of individuals, or institution upon which a person depends betrays the trust of that person or violates their wellbeing. The term was originally used to describe situations in which a child has been violated by a caregiver whom they depended on for survival. (Freyd, et. al., 2007). However, the term has since been extended to describe many other types of situations as well. Because it is a betrayal of trust and can be considered a violation of a wounded partner's wellbeing, trauma due to infidelity is often considered to be betrayal trauma. Wounded partners may not technically depend on their partners for survival, but they may still feel unable to leave the situation for a number of reasons. Additionally, infidelity causes grave harm to attachment and social connections that we as human beings are wired to depend on for survival. This betrayal represents a real threat to the wounded partner's security through attachment, thus triggering a trauma response.

1. Does this information on betrayal trauma relate to your situation? If so, how?

_____
_____
_____
_____
_____

Signs and Symptoms of Betrayal Trauma

The feelings associated with betrayal trauma are intense. A person experiencing betrayal trauma might deal with some, or even all, of the following:

- Shame
- Depression
- Guilt
- Self-blame
- Flashbacks
- Nightmares
- Impaired sleep
- Anxiety
- Fuzzy thinking
- Distrust

- Difficulty concentrating
- Disassociation
- Difficulty expressing or regulating emotions

1. Are you currently experiencing any feelings associated with betrayal trauma? If so, which ones?

_____

_____

_____

_____

_____

The Traumatized Brain

Emotional trauma and PTSD have been shown to cause impairment and even damage to the amygdala, hippocampus, and prefrontal cortex. (Koenigs, Grafman, 2009). The amygdala plays a role in detecting threats as well as activating the appropriate fear-related responses. It also plays a role in attaching emotional significance to memories. Damage or impairment of the amygdala can cause problems such as poor decision-making, emotional dysregulation, and memory problems. The main functions of the hippocampus involve learning, memory encoding, memory navigation, and spatial navigation. Studies have shown that trauma and high levels of stress can reduce the volume of the hippocampus, resulting in deficits in both visual and verbal memory. (Kim, et. al., 2015). The prefrontal cortex contributes to a variety of executive functions, including focus and attention, impulse control, decision-making, and the management of emotional reactions. Traumatic stress can diminish functionality of the prefrontal cortex, making it difficult to make good decisions, regulate emotions, or solve problems. (Arnsten, et. al., 2015).

Also playing an important role here is the autonomic nervous system (ANS). The ANS has two main systems – the sympathetic nervous system and the parasympathetic nervous system. The sympathetic nervous system is associated with the fight/flight/freeze/fawn response to threat and the parasympathetic nervous system helps it calm down. These two systems are meant to work in conjunction with one another so that balance can be achieved in the body. Traumatic experiences can interfere with the balance between these two systems. (Cohen, et. al., 2007).

The good news is that you can play an active role in healing the brain after traumatic experiences. Medications, cognitive behavioral therapy (CBT), neurofeedback, and EMDR (eye movement desensitization and reprocessing) have all been shown to be helpful in treating PTSD and trauma-related issues. Another therapy that can be helpful is Somatic Experiencing.

There are things we can do in our everyday lives to help engage the parasympathetic nervous system and calm down the sympathetic nervous system. If you Google "Somatic Exercises", you will come across a host of simple exercises that can, when practiced regularly, help you return to a more relaxed mental state. The best way to practice Somatic Experiencing exercises is to do them throughout the day, every day. I personally like the ones offered through Arizona Trauma Institute. Their YouTube Channel is: https://www.youtube.com/c/aztraumaorg.

Another great practice, especially for intrusive thoughts, is mindfulness. Practicing mindfulness can help you reduce anxiety and decrease rumination. (Grossman, et. al., 2004). Mindfulness is being aware of one's experience in the moment without judging that experience. A great definition of mindfulness comes from psychologist Scott Bishop, Ph.D.:

"Mindfulness is a nonelaborative, nonjudgmental, present-centered awareness in which each thought, feeling, sensation that arises... is acknowledged and accepted as it is."

For wounded partners who are struggling with resuming sexual intimacy with their mate, mindfulness can be particularly useful. Because we experience our partner's infidelity as trauma, intrusive thoughts often come into our mind when we are trying to engage in sex. Concentrating on our current experience can keep us in the present and help us manage intrusive thoughts. For example, concentrating on the feel of our partner's kiss, arms around our waist, etc. can give us something to focus on, making it less likely that unwanted thoughts will take over.

1. Name at least one thing you learned in this section. Can you see this being helpful to you? How?

_____
_____
_____
_____
_____

There is no doubt about the fact that recovering from the effects of infidelity creates all kinds of uncomfortable moments. Humans are hard-wired to avoid discomfort and pain. We don't like change and studies have shown that we tend to stick to routines, even when making changes would likely improve our lives. (Andreatta, B., 2017). This is often seen as a way of avoiding potential pain. However, other studies have shown that people who are willing to be slightly uncomfortable are able to develop more successful coping skills when life gets challenging and uncomfortable than those who aren't willing to adapt and/or change routines. (Woolley, Fishbach, 2022) (Dugas, et. al. 2019). Being uncomfortable while trying to learn a new skill plays a huge role in improving performance, creativity, and learning. While our partners often struggle with the uncomfortableness of learning new coping skills (especially if addiction is at play), we as wounded partners most often struggle with dealing with uncomfortable feelings. The key word in either case is "struggle".

When we struggle with a particular emotion, we amplify it. Let's take the emotion of sadness for example. Say we feel sad, but we really don't want to feel sad. We may then struggle with this emotion, adding other emotions to it like anger and guilt over being sad. What we've done by struggling with this emotion is actually increased the intensity and number of emotions that we're now struggling with. Instead of just dealing with sadness, we now have guilt and anger to deal with too.

What we *can* do is choose not to waste our time and energy struggling with an emotion that makes us feel uncomfortable. Instead, we can devote that energy to life-giving activities such as spending time with friends, going for a walk, or doing something else that brings us happiness, joy or relaxation.

This does not mean that we necessarily enjoy experiencing that particular emotion, but instead of struggling with it, we make space for it, experience it, and move through it rather than getting "stuck" in that emotional state. This is the essence of the non-judgmental state that happens in mindfulness. When we judge an experience or ourselves, we add unnecessary complications to the situation. A simple way to avoid doing and practice mindfulness is by doing the Expansion Exercise, which is something I learned from Author Russ Harris in his book *ACT Made Simple*. (Harris, 2019). The exercise, designed to help people deal with overwhelming feelings and uncomfortable emotions, has 4 main steps:

1. Observe
2. Breathe
3. Create Space
4. Allow

There are several great videos on YouTube that will help you practice this exercise. Search ACT or Expansion Exercise to find one that is right for you.

1. Are there certain emotions that you struggle with? If so, what are they? Do you think it's important to make room for them? Why or why not?

_____
_____
_____
_____
_____

CHAPTER 3

Roadblocks to Healing

Inconsistency

Possibly the most important ingredient to recovery is consistency. Conversely, inconsistency in recovery is possibly the largest roadblock to healing for wounded partners. It is important that we are always working toward accomplishing our recovery goals and creating stability for ourselves during tumultuous times. Consistency is how we can achieve that. Furthermore, consistency can help fast track improvements that we wish to make in any area of our lives. When we are consistent, we can show ourselves and others that we're serious about our recovery. When we experience the effects of infidelity, we lose trust in our partners, but we can also lose trust in ourselves. When we develop the discipline and self-control it takes to be consistent in our recovery, we can find a new respect and trust within ourselves. Our recovery work will challenge us at every level, so it is important to watch out for the following behaviors/pitfalls that could ultimately move us off track.

The most common pitfalls that we need to avoid when it comes to being consistent and focused on our recovery are:

1. Procrastination

2. Distractions

3. Unclear goals

4. Excuses

5. Fatigue

One of the most common ways that wounded partners can get sidelined when it comes to reaching their recovery goals is exhaustion. This is completely understandable, given the circumstances. That's why it's so important to get sleep during this time. Humans don't function very well without it, and it's easy to get overwhelmed with everything and end up doing nothing when we're tired. Therefore, one of the first things you should develop consistency in is your sleep schedule.

Here are some ways we can develop consistency in all areas of our lives:

1. Develop new, healthy habits

2. Set small, achievable goals

3. Stick to a schedule

4. Use reminders

5. Develop good sleep hygiene

6. Be kind to yourself while you're trying to develop consistency

This last one is especially important. For some of us, consistency comes easily because we've had it in other areas of our lives. For others, being consistent with our recovery is going to be a huge challenge. Don't criticize yourself or be overly hard on yourself while you are learning a new way of being. I love this quote by Brené Brown that reminds us to be kind to ourselves: *"Talk to yourself as you would someone you love."*

Or this one from Jack Kornfield: *"If your compassion does not include yourself, it is incomplete."*

1. What disciplines do you think will be the most important to develop in order to support your recovery? Why?

_____
_____
_____
_____

2. List some strengths that you currently possess that will help you remain consistent in your recovery.

_____
_____
_____
_____

3. Consistency in recovery starts with following a schedule. Make a list of the days and times you will set aside to work on your recovery.

_____
_____
_____
_____

Inconsistency is only one of the roadblocks to healing that we as wounded partners can face. Although this list is by no means exhaustive, here are some of the other most common healing roadblocks that I see in my office:

Denial of the issues

This is a big one. Although a short period of denial can be healthy in that it helps us absorb the shock of a traumatic incident or distressing information, staying there keeps us stuck. When I see wounded partners stay in denial for extended periods of time, it is always because they're afraid of what it means for them to look at the facts. This can be especially damaging in the case of sexual or porn addiction. Addiction issues that remain in the dark tend to get worse over time.

Indulging in emotions we can't afford

While processing our emotions is imperative to recovery, indulging in unproductive emotions can keep us from moving forward. Probably the most common of these is self-pity. Some other common emotions that we as wounded partners can indulge in are self-doubt, indecision, and blame. Don't get me wrong, these things are valid from time to time. However, indulging in them is a mistake because they keep us stuck. They are simply distractions that keep our focus away from what we should be focusing on to move forward.

Grandiosity

This is a term that I borrowed from the amazing psychotherapist and author Terrence Real. In his book *Fierce Intimacy*, Real defines grandiosity as "contempt for others" while he defines shame (the opposite of grandiosity) as "contempt for self". (Real, 2018). Grandiosity is when we hold someone in contempt. (Contempt is defined as the feeling that a person or thing beneath our consideration or deserving of our scorn). In the case of wounded partners, we often hold our wounding partners in contempt out of righteous indignation. (Righteous indignation is a reactive emotion over perceived or real mistreatment). They may deserve to be yelled at, shamed, and punished for what they have done. Unfortunately, this type of behavior on our part turns us into people we don't want to be. Additionally, if we hope to reconcile, treating our partner with contempt is like shooting holes in our own boat. Grandiosity is not productive and can ultimately contribute to the demise of our relationship, even if we want it to work.

Expecting our partner to fix us

I know this was covered earlier in this section; however, it bears repeating. While our wounding partners can do a lot to help our recovery by listening empathetically, expressing remorse, and accepting responsibility, they can't fix us. We must take charge of our own recovery, just as they have to take charge of theirs.

Remaining ambivalent about recovery

Many people think that to be ambivalent means that someone doesn't care about something. This is incorrect. Ambivalence actually means that someone is experiencing equally powerful negative and positive evaluations of a particular problem or subject, creating a "zero sum game" that causes paralysis.

As wounded partners, we can be ambivalent about engaging in recovery. Unfortunately, as long as we are, we'll remain unproductive and stuck. We can also remain ambivalent about whether or not we want to put any effort into the relationship with the partner who wounded us. This is normal, for a time. However, wounded partners who remain ambivalent for an extended period of time tend to get stuck. The good news is that the cure for ambivalence is to pick a direction and head that way. This will likely feel uncomfortable. However, recovery is often uncomfortable, especially in the beginning. Remember, deciding to put effort toward your own recovery or reconciliation with your partner doesn't mean you are accepting their behavior as okay or excusing it.

1. Can you relate to any of the above-described roadblocks to healing? If so, which ones?

_____
_____
_____
_____
_____

2. Take at least one of the roadblocks that you listed above and journal about why you think that it's a struggle for you. List at least one strength or resource that you currently have that could help you in overcoming it.

_____
_____
_____
_____
_____

CHAPTER 4

Safety in Disclosure

Next to ending an affair or stopping the infidelity-related behavior, how couples handle the disclosure process is probably the most important determining factor of whether the relationship can recover. If the disclosure process is riddled with shaming, deception, and a lack of empathy, there's a high likelihood of reinjury to the relationship as well as to the individuals involved.

The goal of disclosure is to get all of the information regarding any infidelity-related behavior out in the open. Full disclosure must happen if reconciliation is to become possible. When there are secrets and lies between people, disconnection and mistrust will likely control the relationship.

One very important variable during full disclosure is the depth and detail of what the wounded partner wants to know. If the wounded partner doesn't want to know certain information, then what is not known by choice wouldn't be considered a secret or a lie. It's important to note that the disclosure process should be driven by what the wounded partner wants to know. However, the wounding partner should not withhold information just because they were not asked exactly the right question. The goal of disclosure on the wounding partner's part should be to become completely honest and transparent in an effort to help mend the injuries caused by their infidelity-related behavior.

When our partners purposely withhold information from us, it is a second betrayal. Not only have they engaged in infidelity-related behavior; now they are deciding what we do and do not get to know about said behavior. We should be the ones to decide what details we need to hear in order to attempt to move towards reconciliation. If we are being asked to forgive and move forward, we are going to have an extremely hard time doing that if we don't know what we are being asked to forgive. Asking a wounded partner to move on while withholding the facts is not only unfair and uncompassionate, but it is profoundly disrespectful.

Disclosure vs Discovery

I would like to briefly talk about the difference between disclosure and discovery and what typically results from both.

True disclosure is a process in which the wounding partner prepares a statement of events surrounding infidelity-related behavior and discloses them to their partner. This process is usually facilitated by a trained professional and is a contained event where all of the necessary information is relayed completely and with compassion. For disclosure to happen and be an effective and sincere means of coming clean, the infidelity-related behavior must cease. Only when the behavior has ceased will disclosure provide a starting point from which the couple can begin to reconcile. Although disclosure can provide a way for the relationship to move forward, it is still an extremely painful event in the wounded partner's life and can negatively impact attachment as well as trust for this partner. However, one of the main benefits of disclosure is that it demonstrates regret and remorse on the part of the wounding partner and shows that they are sorry for their actions and are willing to do what it takes to repair the resulting damage. It also shows that the wounding partner is willing to commit to honesty and transparency in the future, which are crucial components to rebuilding trust. Although disclosure causes injury to the wounded partner, that injury is more like a surgical cut that can heal properly. Conversely, discovery and dribbling disclosure causes a jagged wound that will re-injure the wounded partner time and time again.

Discovery is entirely different than disclosure. It's usually an unplanned event that is not supported by a trained professional and is often marked with conflict, anger, and defensiveness. Discovery can look like the wounded partner finding evidence of an affair or addiction (text messages, phone calls, web searches, etc.) or an admission blurted out during a conversation. Oftentimes, the wounding partner had no intention of telling their partner anything and, in many cases, is still conflicted about ending the affair or other infidelity-related behavior and/or protecting an addiction. Typically, what the wounded partner discovers doesn't give them the full picture of what's going on. Injuries to attachment are aggravated and feelings of distrust and betrayal increase when this occurs. Oftentimes a period of weeks, months, or even years of digging for answers follows and "dribbling disclosure" becomes a serious threat to the survival of the relationship. As opposed to disclosure, the goal of both discovery and "dribbling disclosure" is for the wounding partner to protect themselves from the consequences of their actions by staggering or completely withholding information pertaining to the infidelity-related behavior.

Dribbling Disclosure

As I mentioned previously, the primary goal of disclosure is to get all of the information pertaining to the infidelity-related behavior out in the open. The way in which this happens matters. The term "dribbling disclosure" describes a scenario in which infidelity-related details are staggered, or "dribbled", out over time. I don't advise dribbling out information over time or purposely withholding pertinent information from the wounded partner. I would like to note here that the damage to the wounded partner resulting from dribbling disclosure is similar to the damage caused by discovery, as described above. The reason for this can be found in how deception breaks trust.

To deceive someone means to cause them to believe something that is not true, usually for some self-interested reason. Honesty in a relationship goes far beyond simply not lying. Obviously, lies and betrayal break down trust. However, deception by telling half-truths, gaslighting, or minimizing breaks down trust even further. When someone withholds information from a person who has a right to know the truth, they deprive that person of the ability to make informed decisions regarding their own life. (A concept in psychology known as a sense of agency.) This essentially robs them of personal choice.

When the wounding partner purposely withholds information or tells partial truths, they engage in deception. Typically, the reason for this deception is that they are worried that the relationship will end if they tell their partner the truth. Although this is certainly understandable, it is ill-advised. What usually ends up happening is one of the following scenarios:

1. The wounding partner feels guilty about withholding information and ends up telling the truth in parts over time.

2. The wounded partner senses that they don't have the full truth and continues to press their spouse/partner to learn the details. The pressure for the wounding partner builds, and they end up reluctantly disclosing the hidden information.

If either scenario happens, we have entered into what I would refer to as "dribbling disclosure". This results in the wounded partner being subjected to repeated trauma. This is profoundly damaging for three main reasons:

1. Each new discovery restarts the grieving process. When infidelity is discovered or disclosed, the losses felt are immediate. This initiates the grieving process over what has been lost. When multiple disclosures happen, this compounds the grieving process because each instance of new information creates additional losses that will have to be grieved. One of the biggest losses resulting from multiple discoveries or disclosures is the loss of the ability to believe our partner can be honest and transparent.

2. Each new discovery creates a new injury and compounds a pre-existing one. The discovery or disclosure of infidelity is traumatic to wounded partners. Emotional trauma creates injury to the psyche of the person experiencing it and will result in challenges to their ability to function and cope as they once did. (NIH Library, 2014). Pre-existing injuries are often made worse when new injuries inflict the same area. This holds true for both physical and emotional injuries. Furthermore, multiple disclosures create multiple injuries, which inevitably makes it much harder for the wounded partner to heal overall.

3. Each new discovery further erodes an already-fragile trust. Most wounded partners tell me that, as hard as it is to forgive infidelity, it is even harder to forgive the deception surrounding the infidelity. The fact that a person had a secret life that we knew nothing about can be a hard thing to get over. It's even harder to get over it when someone keeps lying. After a while, we can begin to wonder if our partner is even capable of telling the truth. This can seriously affect our willingness to move forward with the relationship. Additionally, when our partner repeatedly lies to us, they send us the message that they are more interested in protecting themselves than they are in caring for our broken heart.

1. After reading this section, do you think you've experienced discovery or disclosure? Why do you think this?

_____
_____
_____
_____
_____

2. Do you think you have the information you need in order to move forward with the process of reconciling with your partner? Why or why not?

_____
_____
_____
_____
_____

I would like to add here that, many times, both discovery and disclosure are processes as opposed to one-time events. Typically, unless the wounding partner is prepared to come clean the first time, it takes about 4-6 weeks to get all of the necessary information out into the open. That being said, I have seen it take much longer in some cases, especially when the wounding partner isn't willing to do what it takes to reconcile. I would also like to note that this is a process that many couples can, unfortunately, stay stuck in. It's completely normal for a wounded partner to ask the same questions repeatedly for a while. Please keep in mind that until you can move past this, other parts of the recovery journey will remain on hold.

Our Part in Creating Safety

This is probably the most unpopular topic of everything I have to say to wounded partners, but I would be remiss if I didn't include it. Please don't take offense to what I have to say on the subject of safety. I fully understand how you have been betrayed, and I empathize with the intense suffering that betrayal causes. However, in the interest of recovery, I must stress the need for you as the wounded partner to analyze your words and actions to see if they might be considered unsafe.

The reason for this is that, regardless of the circumstances, nobody likes to engage someone who acts in an unsafe manner. In particular, if your goal is reconciliation, please understand that your partner will likely be hesitant or even reluctant to engage you in recovery in any meaningful way if they perceive that your main goals are to punish them and use them as an emotional punching bag. Although they were the one who initially broke your trust, they also have to trust you in order to continue to share their thoughts and feelings with you. True reconciliation requires intimacy, and intimacy requires vulnerability. Your partner will not want to become vulnerable if they perceive you to be unsafe. I realize that this might seem unfair to many of you, and it may, in fact, actually be unfair. However, the rules surrounding a functional, healthy relationship don't change just because infidelity has entered the mix. Yelling, calling names, shaming, and other types of unsafe behavior will have the same effect on your partner now as they would've had prior to the infidelity. A lack of safety, for any reason, can mean the death of a relationship.

If you, as a wounded partner, are acting in unsafe ways, I urge you to get help and become accountable for your behavior. This is not to say that you can't feel angry, hurt, confused, or all of the many other feelings that come with betrayal. Your experience and the feelings that come with it are completely valid. What becomes problematic when it comes to reconciliation is the way in which we behave when we experience intense emotions.

1. How do you feel about this section of the book? Can you see how becoming a safe person could benefit you or your relationship? If so, how?

_____
_____
_____
_____
_____

Our partners have done plenty to make us feel unsafe. First and foremost is the fact that the infidelity shattered our sense of safety, belonging, and security. Another way that they can make us feel unsafe is with "dribble" disclosure or by purposely withholding important details from us about the infidelity-related behavior. Minimizing, defending, and blaming are other ways that our partners can make us feel unsafe, causing us to question whether it is a good idea to try to reconcile with them. That being said, there are several ways that wounded partners can make the relationship an unsafe place to be as well. These behaviors, when done on a regular basis, can ultimately contribute to a situation in which the wounding partner decides not to participate in the process of reconciliation. Here are the most common ones that I see in my office:

Shaming

While it is completely normal and healthy to express how someone's unfaithful actions have affected us, it's not advisable to shame them. Shaming, by definition, is the act or practice of attempting to embarrass a person by drawing attention to their offense. (Collins Dictionary). Shaming can be public or private. A lot of what goes on between partners is private, although I have seen instances of shaming take place in front of family members, co-workers, friends, and even casual acquaintances. In my experience, when wounded partners shame their unfaithful partner, it's usually an attempt to get them to be sorry for bad behavior, change their behavior, get them to empathize, or flat out punish them. The wounded partner mistakenly thinks this will end up drawing them closer somehow. While shame can be a powerful motivator for behavior change, it is important to understand that it does more harm than good. The feeling of shame activates the stress hormone cortisol, which is a component of the body's fight or flight mechanism. Shame challenges a person's identity and tells them that there's something wrong with them. Therefore, shaming is far more likely to elicit aggressiveness, defensiveness, or withdrawal than a positive, nurturing response. (Stuewig, et. al., 2010).

1. Have you ever been shamed by someone? What did they say to you that shamed you? How did it feel? Did it help you or harm you?

_____
_____
_____
_____
_____

2. Are you currently shaming your partner for their actions? What are your reasons? What could you do or say instead?

_____
_____
_____
_____
_____

Unbridled Anger

Anger is a very common emotion felt by wounded partners. Anger is part of the grieving cycle and a normal response to betrayal, injustice, pain, and loss. It helps tell us something is wrong and can be a very strong motivator for us to create change and defend ourselves in dangerous situations. Feeling angry isn't wrong. However, keeping check on how we act and what we say when we're angry is crucial to the recovery process. Anger becomes a problem when it starts harming us and others around us. Outward aggression such as yelling, screaming, slamming doors, calling names, or being physically violent have no place in a recovering relationship. Inward aggression, such as self-harming, negative self-talk, or cutting ourselves off from the world are also unhealthy forms of anger. Additionally, passive-aggressive forms of anger such as using the silent treatment, sulking, or being sarcastic can be relationship killers as well.

If you think you might have an issue with unbridled anger, I urge you to get some help and accountability for it. Make a commitment to becoming and remaining a safe person by taking timeouts before speaking, going for walks to release the tension, and getting plenty of exercise and rest so that you can manage your feelings to the best of your ability.

1. Are you currently struggling with unbridled anger? In what way(s)? Write down some things that you can do to help get this under control.

_____
_____
_____
_____
_____

Controlling Behavior

Whether or not we exhibited controlling behavior before the infidelity or not, the anxiety produced by betrayal can create or exacerbate controlling behavior. Please understand that I am not talking about things a wounding partner who is trying to escape accountability might object to and label as "controlling". Maintaining clear boundaries, giving an ultimatum that the infidelity-related behavior stop, putting trackers or filtering software in place, or just generally expecting that the wounding partner engage in recovery behavior are completely appropriate responses to betrayal. It's okay to expect that the one who wounded us will now do everything they can to make sure it won't happen again. Expectations around the wounding partner taking responsibility for their actions and being accountable moving forward don't qualify as controlling behavior.

What I am referring to is over-the-top behavior such as calling someone at work every hour, constantly monitoring recovery by snooping through their personal belongings, stalking, eavesdropping, or just generally being in a hypervigilant state of suspicion over every word and every action. These types of behaviors border on harassment and aren't conducive to a healthy relationship. It is important to remember that we can't control our partner's actions now any better than we could before the infidelity occurred. Additionally, a person has to want to reconcile and do the behaviors that support recovery – we can't do it for them or force them into it. Although accountability is crucial in a relationship, harassing someone with intimidating or intrusive behavior will do nothing to solve the issue.

1. Do you feel that the expectations that you have regarding your partner's recovery are appropriate? Why or why not?

_____
_____
_____
_____
_____

At the end of the day, if a relationship is to truly recover from infidelity, each person must take responsibility for their actions. Taking responsibility for one's actions requires a realization that we play a part in how our relationships function and have some degree of responsibility in the outcomes of those relationships. This doesn't mean that we take responsibility for our partner's recovery or actions, but it does mean that we don't blame our partner for any bad behavior exhibited on our part. We need to correct what's ours to correct and leave the rest.

Here are some ways that we can take responsibility for our actions:

- Recognize and own up to any part you have to play in what is occurring within your relationship

- If you hurt your partner with your words, examine how you might say things differently the next time

- Don't excuse your behavior by citing your partner's infidelity

- Take the initiative to do your part in helping the relationship heal

I would like to add here that, for many of us, accepting responsibility for our actions isn't as much of a problem as accepting too much responsibility for the actions of others is. Please don't confuse accepting responsibility with taking on responsibility that others are trying to put onto you because they don't want to accept their own. This type of scenario is much more related to boundaries than it is to accepting responsibility and being a safe person. The subject of boundaries is covered in the next section.

1. Are you currently exhibiting any behaviors that could potentially be destructive to your relationship? If so, what are they?

_____
_____
_____
_____
_____

2. How are you going to change those behaviors and/or become accountable for them?

_____
_____
_____
_____
_____

CHAPTER 5

Asking Questions

When there has been infidelity of any type in a relationship, the questions are many. Regardless of infidelity type, questions center around who the behavior was with (in the case of emotional and sexual affairs), how and when the infidelity-related behavior began, details surrounding the behavior, if the behavior has ended or is ongoing, what the wounding partner is willing to do to make sure it doesn't happen again, and the "why" questions. We will take a closer look at these 6 categories in the pages ahead, but first I would like to address how communicating mindfully can help you when you are in the asking questions phase.

Communicating Mindfully

Without a doubt, dealing with the aftermath of infidelity brings on some of the most intense emotions that wounded partners can experience. Previously, I discussed the role of the sympathetic nervous system when it comes to how partners experience the trauma of betrayal. If you remember, the sympathetic nervous system is responsible for the fight/flight/freeze/fawn response to threatening situations. This response can come into play when partners begin to ask questions as well. It is not uncommon for a wounded partner to feel an adrenaline rush after suddenly thinking of a question that they need to ask their unfaithful mate. This surge of adrenaline, however, is a clear sign that the question that came to mind has likely triggered a feeling of unsafety and the sympathetic nervous system has kicked in to prepare the body for a response to a perceived threat. Real or imagined, the sympathetic nervous system will respond the same to this trigger. (Harvard, 2020).

As a general rule, it is not a good idea to ask your partner questions in the heat of the moment. I advocate for a 24-hour evaluation period as well as doing exercises that engage the parasympathetic nervous system (such as somatic experiencing) prior to asking any questions. My advice is for you to write down any questions you may have and commit to not asking them for 24 hours. Additionally, I advise asking yourself the following questions about each question to determine whether or not they truly need to be asked:

1. Why do I want to know the answer to this question?

2. Will the answer to this question help me recover? (yes or no)

3. If yes, how will the answer to this question help me recover?

If the answer to a particular question will not help you recover in any significant way, I advise that you strike that one from your list of questions.

Communicating mindfully first requires that you understand yourself and become clear on your thinking and feelings around each question. If waiting a while to ask a question means that we can ask it in a calm, non-destructive manner, it will be better for us and our relationship in the long run to do so.

Now, let's take a closer look at the 6 categories of questions described above:

1. Who Was it With?

It is only natural to want to know with whom your partner has been unfaithful (in the case of either sexual or emotional infidelity). However, I urge you to use caution here. Asking questions pertaining to "who" is useful when it comes to sexual or emotional affairs that have happened within your "circle of safety" (people, places, and things that are a part of your life), while asking these questions about someone you don't know can cause more harm than good. The reason for this is that asking questions about someone you don't know often causes natural curiosity to kick in. I've seen partners get stuck for months looking up pictures of people they don't even know. This often leads to unfair comparisons and using their energy to beat themselves up about perceived shortcomings compared to the other person(s). Additionally, partners often waste precious emotional energy on seeking information about total strangers that would be better spent on themselves and/or on their relationship. Finding out what an affair partner looks like, what their hobbies are, etc., while tempting, is unproductive. Ask yourself: what can I possibly know about this person that would make any difference to the situation with my partner?

A better question to ask your partner up front would be, "Do I know this person?" If the answer is yes, then I recommend following up with a question around who the person is. Knowing who the person is makes a lot more sense if you've established that you know them first because it becomes important to understand if they're in the "circle of safety" that I alluded to earlier. Your circle of safety includes people such as family, friends, neighbors, and possibly even co-workers or people you work alongside at church or other functions. It can also include buildings, vehicles, etc. that are a part of your life. People or things in this circle present a more complex issue for a wounded partner because more than one betrayal has taken place: betrayal from the partner as well as betrayal from someone close to you and/or in a place that you personally utilize. Additionally, a lack of knowledge as to who this person or what this place is can cause a situation in which you inadvertently have ongoing contact with someone who has had an inappropriate relationship with your partner or a place where betrayal happened. This can be an extremely unsafe and violating experience.

1. Do you have any questions you need to ask that fall under this category? If so, list them here. Apply the 24-hour rule and ask the set of 3 questions listed previously before asking these questions.

_____
_____
_____
_____
_____

2. How and When Did It Begin?

In order to begin to comprehend what has happened, it is important that you understand the circumstances surrounding the infidelity-related behavior. The answers can vary depending on the nature of the infidelity. Typically, infidelity through pornography or infidelity through withholding (IA) is something that wounding partners carried into the relationship themselves. In my experience, most of these behaviors started long before the wounded partner ever entered the picture.

Here are some examples of appropriate questions to ask:
- When did the affair start?
- How did the affair start?
- Who initiated the affair?
- How long have you been viewing pornography?
- How did you start viewing pornography?
- How long have you been aware that you've been withholding love from me?
- Were you aware that you had an issue with this prior to our relationship beginning?

These are only some examples of the many questions that could be asked in this category. Again, I recommend that you write any questions pertaining to "how and when" here in this section and wait at least 24 hours before asking them.

1. Do you have any questions that you need to ask that fall under this category? If so, write them here. Apply the 24-hour rule and ask the set of 3 questions listed previously before asking these questions.

_____
_____
_____
_____

3. Details of the Infidelity-Related Behavior

This category can be tricky. You want to keep in mind that, while it is important to understand the basic outline of the infidelity-related behavior, too many details will create unnecessary triggers that you don't need. Renowned psychologist Esther Perel has a good list of questions that offer a helpful guide to the questions a wounded partner may want to ask regarding the details of infidelity.

Examples of good questions to ask are:
- How often did you meet this person?
- How often did you have sex?
- Was protection used?
- How often are you viewing pornography and masturbating?
- Why do you feel that it's acceptable to withhold from me?
- Did it ever occur to you that I was suffering from your withholding?
- Did you ever reveal details about me or our family?
- Where are you accessing pornography?
- Where did you find people to have an affair with?
- How much money have you spent on these activities?
- How much time do you spend on this weekly?
- Are you keeping any mementos?
- How did you contact this person/these people?

The list of questions in this category is endless. Please realize that you will likely never understand everything about your partner's activities. The goal here is for you to understand enough of the basic idea of what went on to make informed decisions regarding your future.

I would also like to give you an idea of the types of questions that are what I refer to as "danger zone" questions. These questions, when asked and answered, can re-traumatize an already-wounded partner as well as lead to an increase in intrusive thoughts and triggers.

- Questions pertaining to specific sex acts, positions, etc.

- Questions pertaining to certain locations that might create a trigger for you later on (i.e. specific hotels, cities, etc.)

- Questions regarding details such as hair color, body part sizes, etc.

- Questions pertaining to "dirty talk"

- Questions pertaining to whether they preferred the affair partner's sexual performance to yours

- Questions like, "What do they have that I don't have?"

Remember, the infidelity is not about you. This is about them and their poor choices. You did nothing to deserve this. Asking questions that might lead you to feel bad about yourself or blame yourself somehow won't help you. Your partner could have chosen other ways to behave and, instead, chose to act unfaithfully. Put the blame where it belongs.

1. Do you have any questions that you need to ask that fall under this category? If so, write them here. Apply the 24-hour rule and ask the set of 3 questions listed previously before asking these questions.

_____
_____
_____
_____

4. Is the Behavior Ongoing?

In the work I do, I have found that whether the wounding partner is willing to end the infidelity-related behavior is the number one determining factor as to whether a couple will reconcile or not. As noted earlier, since true recovery within a relationship is contingent upon how seriously both of the people in that relationship take their individual recoveries, it stands to reason that relationships fail when the wounding partner isn't able or willing to change their ways. Failure to reconcile can also happen if the wounded partner simply isn't able to recover from the betrayal.

In my experience, most wounded partners want to know if there is any infidelity-related behavior that's ongoing. Here are some helpful questions to ask:

- Has the affair ended? If so, when did it end? Who ended it?
- Are you still in contact with the affair partner? If so, how do you communicate?
- Do you love this person?
- Do you still look at pornography? When was the last time you looked at pornography?
- Do you intend to end the infidelity-related behavior?
- If you haven't ended the behavior, why not?

These are just a few of the questions that you might have regarding your partner's intentions and activity.

1. Do you have any questions that you need to ask that fall under this category? If so, list them here. Apply the 24-hour rule and ask the set of 3 questions listed previously before asking these questions.

_____
_____
_____
_____
_____

5. Future Intentions

When considering reconciliation with an unfaithful partner, it's important to understand what safeguards they have put in place to help ensure that this behavior won't happen again. If you discovered your partner's infidelity-related behavior, then they won't likely have had time to think about what they should do to get and stay in recovery. In this case, you can ask questions about what they are willing to do instead. Here are some good questions that you can ask:

- Have you been STD tested? If not, are you willing to do so?
- Do you still want to be with the other person?
- Do you still want to look at pornography?
- Do you still want to withhold yourself from me?
- What are your reasons for telling me?
- Do you hope we can reconcile?
- Are you being completely honest?
- Is there anything I haven't asked that you should tell me? (This is a particularly great question because it highlights the fact that information, when withheld, is dishonesty and should be considered another form of betrayal)
- What steps have you taken to block your access to this person, to the porn, etc.?
- Are you willing to join a recovery group?
- Are you willing to do an intensive or couple's workshop?
- Are you willing to take a polygraph test?
- Do you feel guilty?

1. Are there any questions that you need to ask that fall under this category? If so, list them here. Apply the 24-hour rule and ask the set of 3 questions listed previously before asking these questions.

6. The "WHY" Questions

The answers to this category of questions are often the most disappointing and frustrating for wounded partners. Understanding the reason (or reasons) for infidelity seems so key to putting our lives back together, yet many of the answers to "why" elude us. One of the primary reasons for this is that wounding partners rarely know why themselves, at least in the beginning stages of recovery. This is especially true in the case of sex/pornography addiction as well as intimacy avoidance.

Early on, unfaithful partners typically have very little insight into their own behavior. One of the main reasons for this is that, in order to commit betrayal, they had to justify their behavior in their own minds first. This typically leads to several layers of denial that will have to be worked through during recovery. Additionally, someone who has been unfaithful may not feel great about themselves. Poor self-image can lead a person to become defensive when questioned because they're afraid of what the answers might say about them.

Denial and justifications are especially prevalent where addiction is concerned. In order to support the addiction, the unfaithful partner had to compromise themselves and others around them. Many addicts feel intense shame about their behavior, and acknowledging that behavior, especially in the beginning, can be extremely difficult for them. In my experience, IAs and porn addicts tend to have a marked lack of empathy as well. This is especially hard for a wounded partner who needs to know that their partner understands how they've been hurt and cares about it.

Lack of empathy is a sign of emotional immaturity, and addicts and intimacy avoidants are typically less mature than they should be. Emotional maturity develops, in large part, when we must find healthy ways to deal with intense and/or unpleasant emotions. People mature emotionally when they have to struggle to find a resolution within themselves or when they seek trained professionals to help them grow. (Lester, 2021). When someone has an addiction to sex or pornography or even to withholding themselves from their partner, they turn to the addiction time and time again to soothe themselves. In many instances this addictive behavior becomes their primary coping mechanism for all of life's ups and downs. They don't have to deal with life on life's terms and overcome problems because the addiction masks the feelings and gives them an alternative. This leaves them emotionally immature and unable to handle things such as conflict, criticism, and changes that they have no control over. It also leaves them with a lack of self-reflection because of the layers of denial it takes to stay in addiction. The very nature of addiction is to "numb out" or escape emotions. As addiction progresses, it muddies that person's thinking and makes it difficult to evaluate their own behavior. Asking someone with little to no self-awareness to explain to you why they did something will, more often than not, lead to frustration.

If this describes your situation, I want to tell you that I can relate to the pain that you are in. I also want to give you hope that, as your partner moves through recovery, they will emotionally mature and gain empathy in the process. The work done in recovery is all about self-reflection, which can develop very quickly once addiction and "numbing out" behavior is removed. My best advice to you is that you join a support group and/or see a trained professional that can help you work through some of the "why" questions that your partner isn't currently able to answer.

I most often see wounded partners get stuck in the questioning stage of discovery around the "why" questions. Although it can be helpful to understand why someone did something, it can be highly frustrating when they say that they don't know why or when their answers don't make much sense. Many times, we as wounded partners simply have to come to the realization that we may never fully understand our partner's reasons for doing what they did. In order to move forward, we might have to accept the fact that we may never be fully satisfied as to why something happened the way it did and that our partner's confounding behavior will remain, to a point, somewhat of a mystery.

A caveat that I feel is worth mentioning is that many wounding partners will ongoingly use "I don't know" as a way of avoiding answering tough questions. If your partner has been in recovery for more than 3 months, and their answers as to "why" haven't improved, they may be using that as an excuse. It could be an indication that they a.) aren't very serious about their recovery or b.) need more stringent accountability partners, sponsors, or counselors/coaches because they aren't being challenged enough.

1. Do you feel that your partner is able to adequately explain why they did what they did? If not, can you think of something you could do in order to help you understand better? What could you do?

_____
_____
_____
_____

2. Do you have any questions that fall into this category? If so, what are they? Apply the 24-hour rule and ask the set of 3 questions listed previously before asking these questions.

_____
_____
_____
_____

CHAPTER 6

Meanings, Handling Suspicion, and Polygraph

I want to address another way that wounded partners can get stuck in the questioning phase of discovery/disclosure, and that's through assigning meanings. What I mean by "assigning meanings" is a scenario in which the wounding partner has explained their behavior to the best of their ability and the wounded partner refuses to accept it and, instead, assigns a different significance to the infidelity-related behavior. This can take place even after the wounding partner has done recovery, polygraphs, etc. and has shown that they are not only willing to change but are committed to ongoing change.

When I see this type of partner in my office, they are usually frustrated. They might say things like, "I don't know what's wrong with me! Why can't I move on?" This type of being stuck has nothing to do with an unwillingness to give their heart again or to forgive. It has a lot more to do with the fact that they are assigning meanings to their partner's past actions that are based on their own thinking as opposed to understanding how their partner thinks/used to think. I call this disparity "relationship thinking" versus objectification.

The foundation of relationship thinking is that everyone— from the parking lot attendant to co-workers to their partner—has intrinsic value. Because of this value, the relationship thinker wouldn't dream of violating or taking advantage of someone. It doesn't even cross their mind. It also doesn't cross their mind that other people might not see things this same way. However, especially in the case of addicts, not all people view others as having intrinsic value.

Most addicts and intimacy avoidants/anorexics tend to view life, and people, in an operating system that lends itself to seeing people as objects. To a lesser extent, many partners who cheat also slip into this way of viewing others. The foundation of this type of thinking is that "someone only has value if they're doing something for me". When the addict is acting out in their addiction, or when the cheater is cheating, they are not thinking of their partner's value. They are thinking of their own gratification and justifying their actions. They also view themselves as objects as well. There are several reasons for this. One is that it may have been taught to them in their family of origin. Many parents treat their children in this way; giving the child praise and love when they have done something for them and removing love and praise when the child acts up. The result is that the child learns that they have no value unless they have good performance. Abuse, abandonment, and neglect can also teach a child that they aren't valuable, and they might carry this idea that people don't have much value into adulthood. Finally, objectification of people is a sign of emotional immaturity. For example, if you ask a child why they love their mom or dad, their answer will likely be stated in terms of what mom or dad does for them. (I love my mom because she makes me cookies. I love my dad because he plays catch with me). This type of thinking is normal for a child, but we're meant to grow out of it as we age. Unfortunately, abuse, neglect, and addiction stunt emotional growth and remaining in a reality where people are no more than objects is evidence of this.

If you view your partner's actions within the confines of relational thinking, or seeing the value of others, you may become stuck as to why you think that they did what they did. It would be better for you to assign meanings that line up with how people act when they see others as objects instead. Otherwise, you may always interpret your partner's actions as deeply meaningful from a relationship perspective. Although wounded partners may get stuck for a short time while they are trying to wrap their heads around the fact that their partner is using people as objects, the ones who get stuck in relational meaning tend to stay there much longer.

Here are some examples that I've seen of relational meanings being placed on actions based in objectification:

Action	Relational Meaning	Possible Meaning if Objectification is Present
Flirting	They like that person better than me. I'm not attractive.	This builds their ego.
Sexual infidelity (especially affairs that last for months or years)	They loved that person. They don't love me.	It was free, easy sex.
Intimacy avoidance	I need to show more love. They don't love me. I'm not valuable.	They're protecting themselves and staying in control.
Gaslighting	I must be mistaken. I don't understand my mate. I don't comprehend the true nature of things.	They're willing to confuse you to take the spotlight off of their bad behavior.
Pornography	They aren't attracted to me. I'm ugly. I'm fat.	They don't see people; they see body parts. They feel entitled to see what they want when they want it.
Lying	They don't care about me.	They don't want a hassle, so they think it's okay to lie.
Lack of accountability	I'm not important to them.	They want to escape the consequences of their actions.

1. Are you willing to accept that your partner may have been thinking differently about things than you do when they engaged in their infidelity-related behavior? Why or why not?

2. Does this section help you make sense of your partner's actions? Why or why not?

3. Are there any of your partner's actions that you're assigning relationship meaning to? What are those meanings? Write them here. What alternative meaning (according to objectification) can you put to those? Write those alongside your relationship meanings.

Handling Suspicion

For wounded partners who don't know if something is going on or not, trying to figure it out can be an agonizing process. We hope our partner will come clean with us, but sometimes we have to investigate in order to protect our safety and wellbeing. While this list isn't exhaustive by any means, here are some signs of possible infidelity:

- **Changes in physical appearance.** Someone involved in a sexual or emotional affair may suddenly become noticeably concerned with making improvements to their physical appearance.

- **Becoming secretive or defensive around phone and computer use.** These days, we use our phones and computers to communicate constantly. This isn't necessarily a bad thing, but if your partner suddenly becomes secretive or defensive around electronic use, it could be a sign that they are communicating with affair partners, escorts, or looking at pornography.

- **Spending more time at work or out and about.** If your partner is suddenly unavailable, it could mean that they are spending time engaging in infidelity-related activities. Being too busy to spend time with their partner is also a strategy of intimacy avoidants to keep distance between themselves and their partner.

- **Being unreachable.** If you frequently can't reach your partner, this could be a sign of infidelity.

- **Changes in sex.** If your partner suddenly seems uninterested or is suddenly asking you to perform sex acts that are out of the norm, this could be a sign of infidelity and/or porn usage. Also, a common tactic of IAs is to withhold sex, become critical before and after sex, or stay distant during sex.

- **Hostility or criticism.** Unfaithful partners need to rationalize their actions, and a way they can do this easily is to put the blame on you and/or find fault in you. IAs are especially prone to keeping distance between themselves and their partner using ungrounded or ongoing criticism.

- **Lack of communication.** Emotional connection is not high on the priority list for an unfaithful partner. IAs withhold their thoughts and emotions from their partners in order to maintain distance and cause pain.

- **Your gut tells you something is wrong.** I am always amazed at how spot-on wounded partners can be about infidelity-related behavior, even when there's no proof. If your gut is telling you something is amiss, listen to it.

Where to Look

The best way to find out if your partner is being unfaithful is to have an open, honest conversation with them and ask them outright. However, if you suspect infidelity and your partner isn't talking, it is okay to look for proof in order to protect yourself. Here are some places where you might find evidence:

- **Search engine history.** Since technology is so often used for infidelity-related behavior, this is a good place to start.

- **Phone records.** This is another form of technology that might tell you something.

- **Bills.** Credit card statements are another place you can look for unusual expenditures.

- **The car.** Hiding places can include under the floor mats, in the glove compartment, or behind the visor. Any compartment can hold secrets.

- **Dresser or closet.** You might find something here quite easily, especially if your mate is aware that you never look.

- **Cloud services.** Unfaithful partners can use digital cloud services to hide videos and media files.

- **Phone locations.** If your partner has been visiting unusual locations, you can find out more about what these are by using tracking software.

- **Emails.** Various methods can be used to find hidden email accounts. Using a "people search site" is one way to quickly locate hidden emails. If you have someone's phone number, you can usually find someone's hidden social media accounts as well. It is important to note that it is typically illegal to read someone's emails without their permission, but you can still check for hidden email accounts.

Honestly, I dislike even writing this section; however, there are times when it becomes necessary for you to take matters into your own hands in order to protect yourself. I don't advocate for suspicious partners to treat their mates like criminals or invade their privacy. However, I don't advocate for partners to stay in the dark; possibly putting their health and safety at risk, either.

1. How did you feel when reading this section? Do you currently have unconfirmed suspicions? If so, what are they?

_____
_____
_____
_____
_____

Polygraph

As I close this chapter, I would like to briefly discuss the role of polygraph in recovery and disclosure. If you are interested in more information about the polygraph process, check out our book *Rebuilding Trust,* which outlines the therapeutic polygraph process in detail. Although polygraphs aren't completely reliable, which is why the results are not allowed as evidence in court hearings, they can still be a useful tool. When used correctly, a polygraph can help a couple reach the truth, hold wounding partners accountable, and provide a foundation on which trust can be built.

First, I would like to talk about two types of polygraph tests—criminal and therapeutic. If you're going this route, please be clear that criminal polygraphs are not appropriate for the purposes of verifying truth around disclosure. The main reason for this is that polygraph examiners that aren't trained in therapeutic disclosure, infidelity, and sexual or porn addiction will tend to treat the person taking the polygraph as a criminal. Criminal polygraph examiners tend to ask "gotcha" questions that make the subject nervous. While this may work when dealing with criminals, it actually undermines a therapeutic disclosure process because it makes the subject nervous which, in turn, can cause them to flunk the polygraph even if they have been truthful.

The way we use polygraph examinations at Becoming Well is to verify that the information given to the wounded partner during the disclosure process was truthful and complete. Our process for disclosure includes the following:

1. The wounding partner works with a coach to get all of the necessary information on paper.

2. The wounded partner works with a coach to develop a list of appropriate questions.

3. A date is set for disclosure, where the wounding partner will relay the information related to any infidelity-related behavior to the wounded partner.

4. Disclosure takes place, facilitated by at least one coach. The wounded partner is allowed to ask questions and the wounding partner is instructed to answer them without defending. The coach will ensure that all information contained in the disclosure has been disclosed.

5. Once the information is out in the open, a polygraph examination date will be set. Once the polygraph has been administered, the information regarding pass/fail will be sent to the coaches.

6. A follow-up appointment will take place in order to go over the polygraph results. If the wounding partner passes the polygraph without exception, this information will be relayed to both parties prior to the follow-up appointment.

CHAPTER 7

Boundaries

What is a boundary?

The term "personal boundaries" has been circulating for the past several decades. It was popularized by self-help authors in the mid 1980's and was used as a metaphor to describe actions that are "in bounds" and "out of bounds" in terms of what a person will and will not tolerate. The word "boundary" is defined as a line that marks the limits of an area or a limit of a subject or sphere of activity. (Oxford Languages). A personal boundary is an imaginary line that separates people from one another in terms of personal space, feelings, needs, and responsibilities.

Appropriate boundaries are a critical component to maintaining healthy connections to ourselves, our partner, and others around us. Common areas for boundaries include:

- Time management
- Needs
- Accepting (or not accepting) responsibility
- Remaining true to principles
- Sexuality
- The expression of emotions
- Privacy

- Vulnerability
- Taking on the opinions of others
- Personal space
- Identity
- Respect

As you can see from the list above, personal boundaries are really about taking responsibility for your own space and actions.

What a boundary isn't

What a personal boundary is and is not can get a bit confusing. As I wrote previously, personal boundaries are about taking responsibility for our own space and actions. A boundary is not a way for us to try to coerce our partner into behaving the way that we want them to. Believe me, I definitely understand that there are days when we all wish we could do that. However, it is unhealthy for us to try to control or manipulate someone else's behavior. Here are some examples of where the idea of boundaries can go awry:

- Using boundaries to get our way
- Using boundaries in an attempt to guarantee safety
- Using boundaries as threats
- Drawing boundaries for someone else
- Becoming rigid around boundaries
- Creating boundaries around almost everything

1. In your own words, describe what a boundary is and what it isn't.

_____
_____
_____
_____

2. Do you have any areas where you might be misusing boundaries? If so, what are they?

_____
_____
_____
_____
_____

Boundary Types

Boundaries can help protect us from harm. There are six different types of boundaries that apply to most relationships that I would like to highlight here: physical, emotional, sexual, intellectual, material, and time. Let's take a closer look at each one:

Physical Boundaries

Physical boundaries encompass our need for personal space, physical touch, and physical needs such as rest, nourishment, etc. To put it plainly, physical boundaries are about how we want our bodies to be treated. Sharing your physical boundaries with your partner can be helpful to your relationship. For example, if you aren't comfortable with kissing in public, it's important that you share that with your partner. Otherwise, you might end up feeling disrespected if it happens. Other boundaries such as when you need to rest and when you need to be alone are also important to share. Physical boundaries can be violated when someone touches you in unwanted or harmful ways (such as hugging you when you don't want a hug or striking you) and when a person invades your personal space.

Emotional Boundaries

Emotional boundaries are all about respecting feelings and emotional energy. They also let us know where we end, and another person begins. For example, if your partner is feeling agitated and you take this feeling on, you may need to put an emotional boundary in place. You can also limit conversations that take emotional energy by setting a boundary around where and when you talk about certain subjects. Emotional boundaries can be violated when someone criticizes, belittles, or invalidates your feelings.

Sexual Boundaries

Sexual boundaries are vital to any healthy romantic relationship. The idea of sexual boundaries in a relationship encompasses a mutual understanding and respect of limitations and desires between partners as well as overall consent. Sexual boundaries can be violated when we're touched in unwanted ways, coerced or pressured into sexual acts that we're uncomfortable with, guilted into having sex, or are physically forced. Additionally, the act of sexual infidelity violates healthy sexual boundaries in two ways. First, it violates the agreement of sexual exclusivity between partners. Second, it violates the wounded partner's body when the unfaithful partner has sex with them after having sex with someone outside of the relationship. Sexual boundaries can also be violated in open relationships when the rules that the couple agrees upon regarding engaging outside parties aren't followed.

Intellectual Boundaries

Intellectual boundaries are boundaries that we set around our thoughts, beliefs, and ideas. Respecting the thoughts of others, even if they are different than our own, and asking that ours are respected is extremely important. An awareness of appropriate discussion around beliefs, thoughts, and ideas is also encompassed by the idea of intellectual boundaries. Much like emotional boundaries, intellectual boundaries are violated when a person refuses to respect our beliefs, thoughts, and ideas as well as when we don't respect another person's. This can come in the form of belittling, dismissing, or ridiculing.

Material Boundaries

The idea of material boundaries encompasses money and possessions. Healthy boundaries in this area involve setting limitations around how much of what you possess is shared with others as well as with whom it is shared. Material boundaries are violated when someone takes something that belongs to you without permission or uses something you own in ways and with people that you never agreed to. The most common ways material boundaries are violated when it comes to infidelity are when the wounding partner spends money on their infidelity-related behavior, gives gifts to an affair partner, or invites the affair partner into the family home, car, vacation properties, etc.

Time Boundaries

This type of boundary refers to how someone spends their time. We often violate our own time boundaries when we don't set aside the proper amount of time for different areas of our life or don't prioritize our time. Some ways others can violate our time boundaries are by demanding too much of our time or controlling our time by dictating how we must spend it. Another way our time boundaries can be violated is by someone who continually makes us late for things or keeps us waiting.

1. From the list above, name which types of boundaries have been violated through your partner's infidelity (physical, sexual, time etc.). What actions did they take that violated your boundaries?

2. Are there any other types of boundaries that were violated through infidelity that aren't listed above? If so, what were they and how did they happen?

The act of infidelity violates multiple boundaries. For wounded partners, these violations are often felt as losses. The loss of the belief that your partner respected you, the loss of safety in the relationship, the loss of peace of mind. As losses, boundary violations not only need to be identified, but they will also need to be grieved and, eventually, forgiven if reconciliation is to take place. There will be more about the grief cycle as it pertains to betrayal loss and forgiveness later in this book.

1. Have you ever thought of boundary violations as a form of loss? Now that this has come to your attention, can you identify with a feeling of loss due to boundary violations?

2. Make a list of losses you have sustained due to boundary violations. Be sure to include these in the "Counting Your Losses" exercise found later in this book.

Protective and Containment Boundaries

In his book *Fierce Intimacy*, renowned psychologist Terrence Real describes two types of boundaries that are not frequently discussed: protective and containment boundaries. (Real, 2018). He likens these boundaries to the peel and membrane of an orange. The protective boundary is like the tough orange peel. When we have it properly in place, we keep ourselves from being hurt by what others say and do. The containment boundary is like the white membrane that covers the flesh of the orange. When we have this properly in place, we keep ourselves from saying and doing things that might hurt others.

Protective and containment boundaries are especially important in communication. For example, when we as wounded partners need to communicate our emotional pain over our partner's actions, we should be careful that our containment boundary is firmly in place. If we don't do this and simply "blast away" with our words, we run the risk of further damaging an already-fragile relationship. The containment boundary can help us do our part to keep our relationship safe enough for recovery to happen. As wounded partners, it is important to have a strong protective boundary in place as well. When someone tries to communicate in a way that is defensive and/or blaming, we need to be able to decide whether or not to let their comments in. A good question to ask ourselves when someone is communicating this way is, "Is this person saying something about me right now, or are they really telling me something about themselves?" If the first is true, we can take their comments in and evaluate them further. Conversely, if the second is true, we can let their comments go without allowing ourselves to be hurt by them.

Early on in recovery, it is not uncommon for a wounding partner to blame a wounded partner for their infidelity-related behavior. Recovery is a process, and blaming and defensiveness on the part of the wounding partner is often a symptom of shame, guilt, low self-esteem, and denial. It is important for you to have a good protective boundary in place so that you do not end up taking on guilt and shame that are not yours to own.

1. List some areas where stronger protective and containment boundaries would be helpful in terms of communicating with your partner.

_____
_____
_____
_____
_____

Non-negotiables and Ultimatums

Non-negotiables, or "dealbreakers," are important when setting boundaries. Where infidelity is concerned, common non-negotiables include:

- Ending the affair and cutting off all contact with the affair partner (often involves giving proof)

- Willingness to take a polygraph (now and ongoing)

- Willingness to enter counseling or coaching (now and ongoing)

- Willingness to join an accountability group (now and ongoing)

- Willingness to open full access to phone, computer, emails, etc. (now and ongoing)

It is important for wounded partners to understand that it will take a significant amount of time (typically at least 2 years) before a relationship can be completely restored after infidelity. Many changes need to take place in both partners, and this takes time and patience. The wounding partner will need to take a hard look at themselves and put much effort into figuring out their reasons for the infidelity-related behavior without blaming their partner. The wounded partner will eventually have to forgive. This is why I have included the words "now and ongoing" on so many of the items above. It is a process.

Ultimatums are also an important part of the recovery process. You may have heard that ultimatums are unhealthy and can hurt a relationship. Although this is true in many cases, I believe that ultimatums are appropriate when it comes to infidelity. For example, if you have set up healthy boundaries and non-negotiables and your partner keeps crossing them, it may be time for an ultimatum. Ultimatums should be considered last-resort responses to serious boundary violations. Here are some examples of appropriate ultimatums:

- "If you continue the affair, I will end the relationship."

- "If you continue to contact the affair partner, I will end the relationship."

- "If you continue to verbally abuse me, I am moving out."

- "If you discontinue your counseling, coaching, or accountability group I can't trust you, so I need a separation until you resume those things."

The key to using non-negotiables and ultimatums effectively is to use them sparingly. Otherwise, you run the risk of your words falling on deaf ears.

1. What do you think of the idea of non-negotiables and ultimatums?

2. Can you see a use for non-negotiables and/or ultimatums in your current relationship? Why or why not?

3. If you can see a use for a non-negotiable and/or ultimatum in your relationship? Where could you use these?

Boundaries vs Barriers

Healthy personal boundaries support both independence and interdependence. (Interdependence is the dependence of two or more people on each other). They help us to distinguish between our own responsibilities and the responsibilities of others while still allowing us to connect with the people in our lives. Boundaries are essential for relationships because they help others understand how to treat us. They are also important for us as individuals because, without them, we can end up feeling depleted, taken advantage of, and even taken for granted.

A lot of us have a hard time setting boundaries. There are many reasons for this. In my younger adult years, I had a really hard time setting boundaries because I grew up in a home where they were not typically welcomed. My father did not appreciate boundaries unless he was the one setting them. He would mistreat people in our family, including me, and blame us for our reactions to his mistreatment. Sometimes he would even act hurt or feel sorry for himself if anyone spoke up. As a child, the clear message to me was that my feelings were irrelevant when it came to how someone felt like treating me. I also longed for my dad's approval and noticed that he either withdrew from me or criticized me whenever I objected to the way I was being treated. This is a hard thing for a child to take— having to choose between a relationship with a parent and respecting themselves by having boundaries. In an attempt to gain my dad's approval, I chose to lay down my right to have boundaries and, in turn, carried my lack of boundaries into my adult relationships. Other reasons I have seen for a lack of boundaries in partners are people pleasing, fearing the consequences of having boundaries, perfectionism (not ever wanting to let someone down), an upbringing where a parent (or both parents) had a lack of boundaries, and social conditioning — especially in women and people where cultural and/or religious norms demand overperformance in the area of self-sacrifice.

Throughout the process of recovery, partners frequently get the opportunity to practice setting boundaries. This is generally a good thing. However, people who do not have much prior experience in setting them often go overboard and start accidentally creating barriers to intimacy in the name of boundaries. This typically looks like the last two bullet points in the section above where I describe how boundaries can go awry:

- Becoming too rigid about boundaries

- Creating boundaries around almost everything

Both of these definitely applied to me when I was trying to learn how to set boundaries earlier in my life. I began putting boundaries around all kinds of things and became very rigid about them. So rigid, in fact, that I became suspicious of people and would correct them the minute I thought they were even going to put a toe over the line. As a result, the people in my life started feeling uncomfortable around me. My boundaries had become barriers to intimacy. I later came to realize that I was trying to insulate myself from being hurt by setting rigid boundaries around any situation that might prove to be potentially threatening. In essence, I was trying to control the possibility of being hurt by attempting to control the actions of others through my boundaries. What I eventually learned was that I needed to communicate my feelings properly in order to encourage open dialogue with the people in my life. Then, if they refused to respect my boundaries, I would decide what the consequence of that was going to be. We will cover more on that as well as how to set boundaries and consequences later in this section.

1. Could you relate to anything in the story above? If so, what?

_____
_____
_____
_____
_____

2. Do you have a hard time setting boundaries? If so, why do you think that is?

_____
_____
_____
_____
_____

A word about abusive relationships

When someone is in an abusive relationship, boundaries become extremely difficult, if not impossible, to set. It is not uncommon for an abuser to minimize or completely deny the effect that their actions have on their partner. When a partner tries to draw a boundary with such a person, the abuser will often act hurt, sullen, or angry in an attempt to get their partner to back off the limitations that have been set. I have seen this in my office in the form of temper tantrums, the silent treatment, and even Bible verses being flung back in the face of the partner in an attempt to put them back in their place. I have also seen attempts at an apology mixed in with criticism and complaint. An example of this goes something like this:

> *"I'm sorry that you thought I was being controlling. I'll try to do better, but that is going to be hard for me because I feel like you are the one that is always trying to control how I act."*

Yes, the words "I'm sorry" were technically in there, but this type of communication is more about shifting blame in order to get the partner back in line than it is about apologizing for bad behavior.

When this type of manipulation occurs, my best advice is for you to stand your ground and enact an enforceable consequence if the person refuses to respect your boundary. (More on enforceable consequences later in this section). Many partners will have a hard time doing this on their own, so I recommend that you hire a coach or counselor to help you with this process.

If your partner is going beyond verbal manipulation into physical, verbal, emotional, or sexual abuse, I recommend talking to an expert. Help is available 24/7 in the United States through the National Domestic Violence Hotline at 1-800-799-7233. You can also text the word "START" to 88788.

Establishing Boundaries

Boundaries can be set anytime, but it is particularly important to consider establishing some boundaries if you see any of the following signs in yourself:

- You take on the feelings of others
- You're angry a lot of the time
- You feel resentful toward people you care about
- Someone else's bad behavior is costing you emotionally, physically, or otherwise

- You get your needs met by being passive-aggressive, aggressive, or manipulative

- Your fear of abandonment leaves you accepting far less than you deserve

- You say "yes" to others at your own expense

Many people fail to set boundaries because they simply do not know how to do it or are afraid of the outcome. Setting boundaries can sometimes be scary, but it is the best thing we can do for our own safety and mental health. Here is a formula for creating boundaries:

A. Make a list of your personal values. A great time to start putting boundaries in place is any time your values and beliefs are being violated.

B. Take some time to identify what you would like to accomplish by setting a boundary. Journaling and then talking it over with a coach, counselor, or trusted friend can help you process your thoughts and gain a sense of clarity.

C. Make sure that the boundaries being set are reasonable. Again, talking it over with a counselor, coach, or trusted friend can help you gain perspective.

D. Come to accept that stating your boundaries does not guarantee that people will honor them. You can control the boundaries you set for yourself, but you can't control the reactions of others when you do so.

E. Have a straightforward conversation with people in your life about your boundaries and the reasons behind them.

F. Be prepared to hold your ground. Some people will embrace your boundaries and some people will have a hard time with them. Clearly communicating your boundaries is key, but so is being consistent. If you do not act consistently when it comes to your boundaries, you're showing someone how they can slip past them.

G. Be prepared to distance yourself from people who refuse to honor your reasonable boundaries. People who violate your boundaries repeatedly after you've clearly stated them multiple times do not respect you.

1. Take some time to journal here about your personal values.

_____
_____
_____
_____
_____

2. Take some time to journal here about personal boundaries you might want to set and what you hope to accomplish by setting them.

_____
_____
_____
_____
_____

3. List the people in your life who you can trust to give you sound advice about the items on your list and make a plan to talk to them. List specific days/dates you will do this.

_____
_____
_____
_____
_____

When it comes to stating a boundary, I like the DESC method of communication created by Sharon and Gordon Bower as outlined in their book *Asserting Yourself*. The letters DESC break down as follows:

Describe the situation.

Express your feelings and observations about the behavior.

Specify what the ideal outcome would be.

Consequences or compromise. If the behavior persists, explain what the consequences will be. Depending on the situation, a compromise could be appropriate as well. (Bower & Bower, 2004).

Here's an example of how to use the DESC method:

"I notice that when I say something you don't like, you give me the silent treatment. This is hurtful to me, and I don't think it helps our relationship. Ideally, I would like to be able to have an open discussion with you about things that bother me without being given the silent treatment afterwards. If you continue doing this, I'm going to leave the house and do something fun because I don't want to experience that."

Another easy formula for stating boundaries is:

When you (insert behavior)

I feel (insert feeling)

If you (continued behavior)

I will (consequence)

Here's an example of a statement using this formula:

"When you continue communication with your ex-girlfriend, I feel hurt and betrayed. If you continue to communicate with her, I will go to my mom's for a while until you can show me that you've ceased all communication."

These methods are similar to each other and can both be used to effectively communicate your boundaries.

1. Of the two methods above, which one do you find most useful? Why?

_____
_____
_____
_____
_____

2. List one boundary that you would like to set and write out how the conversation would go using one of the methods above.

_____
_____
_____
_____
_____

The role of consequences

You may have noticed that the methods referenced above contain consequences. Consequences play an important role when setting boundaries and should be thought of ahead of time. The proper time to use a consequence is after a boundary has been clearly stated at least once, reiterated at least once, and the person refuses to acknowledge it or honor it.

When I first communicate a new boundary, I prefer to communicate it without using the consequence portion of the formula. I find that the person I am communicating with usually receives what I am saying better without the threat of a consequence. However, I still find it helpful to use the formulas because I can decide on the consequence beforehand if the boundary is repeatedly violated. Using the DESC method above, this is what the statement would look like when leaving off the "C" portion:

"I notice that when I say something you don't like, you give me the silent treatment. This is hurtful to me, and I don't think it helps our relationship. Ideally, I would like to be able to have an open discussion with you about things that bother me without being given the silent treatment afterwards. Can we please agree that you will stop doing this?"

This type of statement with a request at the end gives the person a chance to respond without threat. If they honor my request, that is wonderful. If not, I can always add in the consequence portion when restating my boundary.

Enforceable consequences

When using consequences, make sure that they are something that you have the power to enforce. This means that the consequence: a) doesn't require the other person to do something, b) is something that you are ready and able to follow through on, and c) isn't overly harsh for the situation. **If a consequence for boundary violations requires the other person to do something, it is not enforceable** because you can't control what someone else will and will not do. If you are not prepared to enforce a consequence, pick a different one and then follow up with personal recovery to get to a place where you could enforce the appropriate consequence. By not following through, you are teaching the person that you don't really mean what you say. If your consequences are overly harsh, you may be able to enforce them, but you risk damaging your relationship by building barriers to intimacy.

1. List some appropriate consequences for any of the boundaries you listed above.

_____
_____
_____
_____

2. Are you truly ready to follow through with these consequences? Why or why not?

Common boundary mistakes

Here are a few common mistakes that I see partners make when trying to implement and enforce boundaries:

- Failing to ask for exactly what they want out of fear
- Setting boundaries that they don't believe in or aren't ready to enforce
- Setting boundaries based on what someone else thinks they should do
- Compromising their boundaries as a response to violations (changing boundaries solely based on the fact that the other person refuses to acknowledge, respect, or abide by them)
- Not respecting their own boundaries for themselves (such as not yelling, overeating, etc.)
- Creating too many boundaries
- Withdrawing love from the person they set a boundary with
- Failing to model the boundary themselves

1. Do you see yourself making any of the common boundary mistakes listed above? If so, which one(s)?

CHAPTER 8

Self-Care and Self-Compassion

Self-Care

The term "self-care" encompasses the idea that we need to take care of ourselves so that we can accomplish the tasks that we need to get done. Self-care is part of the answer to how we can effectively deal with stressors in our lives. As wounded partners, we face a wide range of stressors that can seriously impede our ability to maintain our health, do well at our jobs, maintain friendships, and care for our children or other people who depend on us.

Self-care means taking care of ourselves in every area, not just physically. Good self-care includes the physical, spiritual, emotional/mental, social, and financial aspects of our lives. It also involves engaging in active recovery.

Let's take a look at each area of self-care more closely:

Physical: This includes anything pertaining to our bodies. Examples of physical self-care include healthy eating, exercise, drinking plenty of water, good sleep hygiene, and even leisurely activities such as taking a bath or getting a massage. It can also include regularly going to the doctor for health checkups.

Spiritual: It is important to take care of our spiritual side. Self-care in this area can include meditation, prayer, going to church, practicing mindfulness, connecting with God through nature, and reading the Bible or other spiritual literature.

Emotional/Mental: Our emotional and mental health are vital to our wellbeing. Self-care in this area could include practicing emotional regulation through Somatic Exercises (covered earlier), listening to music, engaging in coaching or counseling, reading a good book, listening to helpful podcasts, and making a gratitude list (this one could also be counted as spiritual).

Social: As I wrote earlier, it is important that we do not isolate ourselves during this process. Self-care in this area could include scheduling regular phone calls with supportive friends and family, texting with friends and family, joining a support group and reaching out to the members, spending time with people you care about, attending social events, and going out on dates with your partner in order to provide time for much-needed reconnection.

Financial: Many of my clients describe feeling at a disadvantage because they have chosen to stay at home. For many, this creates an imbalance of power with the wounding partner. While staying at home and caring for the household is an extremely important job that does not get as much respect as it deserves, wounded partners often describe feelings of disempowerment and "stuckness" when it comes to their choice of whether to stay in the relationship because they are completely financially dependent on their partner. If this describes you, some ideas for self-care in this area could include gaining job skills, becoming more involved in the financial aspect of the relationship, or going back to work. Even if you don't feel stuck or disempowered in this area, going back to school, getting a job, or starting a new business for yourself can give you an added boost to your self-esteem.

Engaging in Active Recovery: When it comes to the damage done by infidelity, it is vitally important that we as wounded partners take charge of our own recovery. Reading this book is a sign that you are doing that already. Other ideas could include counseling or coaching, workgroups, reading self-help literature, and attending intensives, workshops, and conferences designed to support your healing.

1. Out of the self-care areas listed above, identify areas where you're strong and areas where you could improve. Write them here.

_____
_____
_____
_____
_____

As you can see, self-care is all about engaging in activities that benefit us. An important thing to realize about self-care is that it is not always about relaxing. In fact, it often requires us to expend energy on healthy activities or engage mentally with things that might feel uncomfortable. The purpose of self-care is to be refueled so that we can deal with the challenges presented by infidelity. As important as it is to identify areas and ways we can take care of ourselves, it is equally important to identify things that can detract from our recovery. Here are some things that self-care is not:

- Being so busy with tasks or helping others that we become depleted

- Overindulging in food or spending

- Using addictive substances such as drugs and alcohol to cope with negative feelings

- Failing to control what we do and say in our anger

- Neglecting our responsibilities

Although many of the activities listed above can seem appealing, they don't do anything to refuel us and can often leave us stressed with feelings of guilt and shame.

Self-care is never as important as when you are facing the aftermath of infidelity. The tsunami of intense feelings and emotional distress that accompany betrayal can leave us feeling seriously depleted. The danger for wounded partners is expending all of our energy to fix the crisis the relationship is facing. The hypervigilance born out of betrayal can become all-consuming. It is important that we take a step back, breathe, and understand that we can't fix everything — as much as we might like to do so. Taking time to focus on self-care is not selfish and will end up helping your relationship in the long run.

1. Are there any activities that you're engaging in from the list above that aren't serving you? List them here.

_____
_____
_____
_____
_____

2. Write a short letter reminding yourself that self-care isn't selfish and is, instead, vital to your wellbeing and the wellbeing of the relationship.

_____
_____
_____
_____
_____

Self-Care Sabotage

In my experience, there are several ways that wounded partners engage in activities in the name of self-care that are actually self-care sabotage. The most common of these are:

- An overindulgence in self-soothing
- Unrestrained gratification of desires (self-indulgence)
- Laziness

Although these things are okay once in a while, an overindulgence in any of them typically sabotages recovery. The hard part is that self-care sabotage can actually feel like self-care in the moment. Self-care only works if you use it to grow — not if you use it to let yourself off the hook or avoid accountability. Here are some helpful questions that you can ask yourself in order to figure out if you're engaging in self-care or self-care sabotage:

- Will this activity support my overall wellbeing or the wellbeing of my relationship?

- Am I willing to let this challenge me, or am I avoiding being challenged?

- Am I isolating myself, or am I just resting up?

- Am I taking an active role in my recovery?

- Am I trying to escape or avoid something by choosing this activity?

- Does this activity connect me to myself and/or others, or do I feel disconnected?

- Am I going to feel better or worse after doing this activity?

- Am I indulging anger or self-pity by doing this activity?

- Will I be better able to do the things I need to do after participating in this activity?

1. Make a list of the activities you do to care for yourself. Do they fall in the area of self-care or self-care sabotage? Why do you think this?

_____
_____
_____
_____
_____

2. On the left of the table, list the activities and behaviors that fell into the self-care sabotage category. On the right of the table, list healthy alternatives to those activities and behaviors.

Another way that wounded partners can sabotage self-care is by simply not setting aside time for it. Waiting for our schedules to "open up" so that we can care for ourselves isn't the best plan of action. Interruptions, unplanned events, distractions, and emotional and physical exhaustion can cause us to constantly come in last when it comes to caring for ourselves. If you want to succeed with self-care, you'll need to prioritize it. Here are some ways you can make caring for yourself a priority:

- Set aside specific times and days for self-care activities
- Wake up a bit earlier
- Break up self-care time into small chunks
- Choose activities that you enjoy, especially when it comes to physical exercise
- Find an accountability partner
- Hire a babysitter if you have children
- Reduce time spent on social media, tv, or streaming services
- Use an alarm as a reminder
- Set specific goals
- Eliminate hurdles to self-care
- Communicate your goals to others
- Plan adequate time for activities (don't be a "time optimist")
- Create boundaries around self-care
- Be assertive with your self-care boundaries
- Engage in brief self-care activities often

Self-Care Worksheet

Activities that support my physical wellbeing

___

Activities that support my spiritual wellbeing

___

Activities that support my emotional/mental wellbeing

___

Activities that support my social wellbeing

___

Activities that support my financial wellbeing

_____
_____
_____
_____
_____

Activities that support my active recovery

_____
_____
_____
_____
_____

Self-Care Worksheet Schedule

Activity	Day	Time

Self-Compassion

"I found in my research that the biggest reason people aren't more self-compassionate is that they are afraid they'll become self-indulgent. They believe self-criticism is what keeps them in line. Most people have gotten it wrong because our culture says being hard on yourself is the way to be."

-Kristen Neff-

The word "compassion" is derived from the Latin word *compati*. The root of the word, *pati*, means "to suffer", while the prefix of the word, *com*, means "with". Hence, the word "compassion" literally means "to suffer with". There are words in the English language such as sympathy, empathy, and commiseration that often get confused with the word "compassion", but they are not the same. The thing that sets compassion apart from all of the others is that it requires that action be taken. Not only does it imply that we are aware of suffering and empathize with it, but also that we feel compelled to do something to alleviate it. Scientists have even begun to map the biology of compassion and have found that, when humans feel compassion, the heart rate slows, oxytocin (the bonding hormone) is released, and the centers of the brain linked to empathy, caregiving, and pleasure light up. As a result, we are compelled to act. (Smith, 2009) (Armstrong, 2017) (Cedars-Sinai, 2019).

Self-compassion isn't much different than having compassion for others. When we have compassion for others, we must first notice that they are in pain. We are then moved by this suffering and are compelled to suffer, or toil, alongside them to ease their pain. The phrases "acts of compassion" and "acts of kindness" are used to describe what we do to show our compassion for others. The same holds true for things we do to show compassion toward ourselves. The problem is that we often fail to complete the first step, which is to recognize and validate our own suffering. Even worse, we often despise ourselves for our suffering because it implies imperfection and weakness.

In order to see ourselves positively, we as human beings tend to inflate our egos. We often compare ourselves to others and put them down in the hopes of boosting our own worth. We tend to criticize or even ignore our flaws and weaknesses or blame others for our difficulties and issues. We also tend to say things like, "Well, at least I'm not as messed up as so-and-so". Americans are especially bad when it comes to comparing ourselves with others. The self-esteem movement was based on the belief that we are all above average and special. Although this might be true occasionally, most of us are basically average. The idea that we are all above-average is flawed because we can't all be special and above-average in everything at the same time. This simple truth inevitably leads to fierce competition. The mindset changed from being okay about being like everyone else to needing to be above others in order to feel that we have value. If we receive input that we are basically average, we take it as an insult. This results in needing to one-up others as well as getting down on ourselves for our flaws, mistakes, and perceived inadequacies. If we eventually do have to admit our shortcomings, we might come to a place of shame or worthlessness. As wounded partners, comparisons are absolutely devastating because we already feel discarded by our mates when they set us aside in their selfish pursuits. The pain is almost unbearable.

The answer to all of this is self-compassion. Author Kristen Neff outlines three distinct requirements for this in her book *Self-Compassion*. They are:

- Self-kindness
- A recognition of our common humanity
- Mindfulness

Let's take a closer look at these three components:

Self-kindness: Self-kindness requires that we be gentle with ourselves when we fail, feel inadequate, and/or suffer. It is the opposite of beating ourselves up with criticism.

A recognition of our common humanity: This is simply recognizing that we are not alone in our suffering. Feelings of sadness, anger, frustration, rejection, and inadequacy are part of the human experience. (Neff, 2015).

Mindfulness: I wrote about this concept earlier in this book. According to Scott Bishop, Ph.D.:

"Mindfulness is a nonelaborative, nonjudgmental, present-centered awareness in which each thought, feeling, sensation that arises ... is acknowledged and accepted as it is."

Self-compassion requires that we take a balanced approach to our emotions, particularly our negative ones. Mindfulness requires that we neither suppress nor exaggerate our feelings but acknowledge and accept them "as is". We can't feel compassion for our pain if we ignore or invalidate it, and we can't remain calm and practice self-compassion if we exaggerate our pain and get swept away in negative reactions to intense emotions.

The good feelings that accompany self-compassion are not dependent on what others think of us, nor are they dependent on how we stack up against the competition. Instead, they come from caring about our pain and doing acts of kindness toward ourselves in order to help alleviate our suffering. Self-compassion comes in at the time we need it the most…when we fail or feel at our most vulnerable and inadequate.

1. Write down at least 2 scenarios in which you felt strong emotions that you perceived as "negative". Write about your experiences without judging them. In other words, just state the facts. An example could be, "I felt furious when someone cut me off on the freeway. I yelled and screamed at them for about 3 minutes afterwards. I think I overreacted. It was in front of my kids."

_____
_____
_____
_____

2. Write down ways that each of the scenarios above are connected to the common human experience. For example, "Many people feel furious when they get cut off. Yelling and screaming are ways humans react to being furious. Even though I think I overreacted, everyone overreacts sometimes especially when they're as stressed as I am. People often make mistakes in front of their kids, especially when they are under stress."

_____
_____
_____
_____
_____

3. Write down some kind words to yourself about the scenarios listed above. For example, "I understand you have been under a lot of stress from the infidelity and are not feeling your best. This is very hard for you, and it is completely understandable that you overreacted. Your kids love you and know that you're a good parent. Maybe you could try talking to them about how everyone makes mistakes sometimes."

_____
_____
_____
_____
_____

Great job! You just successfully practiced self-compassion. 😊

4. List at least 3 acts of kindness that you can show yourself this week.

_____
_____
_____
_____
_____

CHAPTER 9

Betrayal and Grief

"Grief, I say, come in. Sit down. I have tea. There is honey. This will take as long as it takes."

-This Hallowed Wilderness-

How Does Betrayal Cause Grief?

Grief (and the feelings associated with it) is about loss. Typically, we associate the stages of grief with death. The loss felt is tangible and obvious because the deceased person is no longer on Earth. Although betrayal isn't always associated with grief, it is a loss just the same and almost always initiates the grieving cycle. Betrayal is all about loss. Loss of what could have been, loss of what we thought we were sure of, loss of safety and connection. However, unlike death, betrayal creates a special kind of loss because the person is still there, but the trust, safety, and comfort that were felt with them have been lost. This leaves a hole in the wounded partner's heart unlike any other. The wounding partner is typically still in the picture, but the attachment to that person has been lost or, at best, severely damaged.

As I discussed in earlier in this book, betrayal trauma and the ideas behind betrayal trauma theory can help explain why the feelings experienced when infidelity occurs are so powerful. The theory suggests that damage done to attachments, even in romantic relationships, can cause significant and lasting trauma. (Freyd, 1997). Complicating matters is the fact that it is a normal response for a person to pull away from the one who betrayed them.

However, sometimes this isn't feasible or desirable. Trying to restore a severed bond with an unfaithful partner can go against every instinct to protect ourselves that we as wounded partners have, often causing intense discomfort and pain — especially in the early stages of disclosure or discovery. This pain is caused by the losses associated with betrayal. Although attachment can be regained by creating safety once again in the relationship, getting to that attachment requires (among other things) processing our grief.

1. Does it help you to understand how grief and betrayal are related to each other? How can you use this knowledge to help you through the process?

_____
_____
_____
_____
_____

Disenfranchised Grief

Disenfranchised grief (or stigmatized grief) is a term used for a type of grief that society either doesn't recognize or puts a stigma on. There are many examples in our society today of disenfranchised grief. Some of these include:

- "Taboo" death, such as death from suicide, drug overdose, or murder
- Dementia
- Death of an abuser or ex-partner
- Infertility
- Job loss
- Addiction of a loved one
- Other losses not associated with death

Betrayal grief falls squarely into the "other losses not associated with death" category of disenfranchised grief. In our society, grief from death is often considered the most legitimate reason to grieve and we still don't even give people enough time for that. For example, when my father died, the job I had at the time only gave me 3 days off for bereavement and my boss called me in to work for a couple hours on one of those days to deal with an issue. If we are this bad at making room for the feelings and pain of society members for what we consider to be the biggest and most legitimate loss (death), it isn't a surprise that grief from betrayal is often unrecognized and invalidated.

The best advice I can give to you while you struggle with betrayal grief is to seek out the support of non-judgmental people and only talk to those who you truly trust to be supportive and who have earned the privilege of hearing your story. A great many people have been hurt by questions such as, "Why don't you just kick them to the curb?" or, "Why are you even trying to reconcile?" Statements like "I would never put up with that and you shouldn't, either", are just as cutting and unhelpful. Remember, a person standing anywhere other than in your shoes *can't* know what they would or would not do in your situation because they're not you. Perhaps you even thought that you knew exactly what you would do if this were to ever happen to you, only to find that you have reacted quite differently than you ever expected. Stay clear of people who are coming off as judgmental and be careful that you don't judge yourself. No one can know how they would act in *any* situation until the situation is upon them. Seek out the company and counsel of others that are kind, compassionate, and good listeners, and that give you helpful advice and encouragement.

Unresolved Grief

I can't stress enough how important it is to give ourselves the space to grieve fully. By this, I mean allowing ourselves the time and self-compassion necessary to identify our losses, understand how we are feeling, and eventually come to accept what has happened. However, I will mention that one of the most important ways we can show ourselves compassion during this process is to not put expectations on ourselves about how we should and should not feel and get down on ourselves about not being further along in our recovery than we are.

As humans, we tend to use our brains to explain things logically and plan how we are going to act and react to certain situations. One of the things that is particularly difficult for many to accept about grief is that it isn't very logical. To go a step further, not only is it somewhat illogical, but it is often unpredictable as well. The feelings associated with grief often come out at inopportune times and in unexpected ways. I hear stories in my office on a regular basis from clients who were shocked at the intensity of feelings that seemingly came out of nowhere. One client reported suddenly becoming extremely anxious, tearful, and angry in the candy aisle at the grocery store because she suddenly recalled that her husband had once purchased some chocolates for one of his mistresses. This was extremely inconvenient as well as somewhat embarrassing for her. Another client reported that she felt down during important holidays, even though she wanted to be able to enjoy them. Family gatherings triggered reminders of the fact that her partner had been deceiving her throughout the years, often during the times of important gatherings and celebrations.

The unpredictability of grief is problematic in that it lends itself to the urge to "stuff" our feelings and pretend that everything is okay. After all, who wants to climb onto what feels like an extremely unpleasant and unpredictable roller coaster of emotion with no set guidelines for how to get off? Yet this is precisely what we need to do in order to heal. We need to give ourselves compassion, buckle in, and take the ride — understanding that it's okay not to know exactly where our grief is taking us. We can't think our way out of it. We have to walk *through* it. We have to feel it.

Telling ourselves that we are fine, burying our feelings, and going about our lives as if nothing has happened only prolongs our grief. It may seem like we are getting over it, but we are simply sweeping it under the rug. Unresolved, unacknowledged grief has a way of leaking out eventually. Many clients have reported to me that they feel like they are grieving several other losses on top of their losses from betrayal. This is not uncommon. Unresolved grief from prior losses can lie just below the surface and, when that surface is scratched with the pain of betrayal, it comes out with everything else. If we do not take the time to acknowledge and feel our losses, we are only delaying the inevitable.

There are some common responses to unresolved and unacknowledged trauma that I have seen in my clients. Although these can show up anytime during the grief process, in clients with unresolved grief, some or all of them were present prior to the disclosure or discovery of betrayal:

- Refusal to acknowledge or talk about certain losses or certain people
- Prolonged sadness and/or depression
- Constantly needing to be busy and/or distracted
- Isolation or detachment from family and friends
- Digestive issues
- Overindulgence in activities such as eating, drinking, smoking, etc. (This can also show up as undereating and/or risky behavior)
- Refusal to open their heart again for fear of being hurt
- Getting overly angry about or giving overly emotional responses to small events
- Oversleeping or sleeplessness
- Inability or unwillingness to change routines related to someone or something they lost

1. Do you relate to any of the above-listed symptoms? If so, which ones? Were these symptoms present prior to the discovery or disclosure of the betrayal?

_____
_____
_____
_____
_____

2. Do you suspect you may have unresolved grief? Why or why not?

_____
_____
_____
_____
_____

Even if we *seem* successful in constantly tamping our feelings down, we may not actually *be* as successful as we think. Unresolved grief can affect us not only emotionally, but physically as well. I have personally had grief manifest itself in the form of headaches, stomach pain, and sleeplessness. Doctors have cited unresolved grief in instances of increased blood pressure and blood clots. (Mayo Clinic). There is even a type of heart disease known as "broken heart syndrome" linked to it that can have the same symptoms as a heart attack. (Koulouris, et. al., 2010). In addition, severe depression and anxiety, which are not normal symptoms of grief, can also be complications of unresolved grief. (Maercker, et. al., 2017).

1. Have you noticed that reminders of other losses have been coming up for you lately? If so, you may have unresolved grief. Write those losses here. Which feelings are similar to what you feel now? Which ones are different? Are you able to differentiate them?

_____
_____
_____
_____
_____

2. Have you been taking time to grieve? If not, why not? If so, how? Do you think you could set aside some time each day to allow yourself to process your grief? If so, when and how would you do it?

_____
_____
_____
_____
_____

I would like to add here that it is important that we do not try to do this alone. The support of *safe* friends, trained professionals, and a *safe* community of others who understand are more important now than ever. Not only does it help us to normalize what we are going through by hearing the feelings and stories of others, but we can also get the emotional support we need to progress on our healing journey. It can be extremely encouraging to hear from people who are further down the road than we are. It helps us to know that this phase of life is not going to last forever.

1. Do you have the support of friends, trained professionals, and others to help you through this time? If the answer is no, write down some ideas of where you might go to get the support you need. If the answer is yes, do you think you have all of the support you need? What areas (if any) are lacking?

_____
_____
_____
_____
_____

2. Are you comfortable with the idea of getting support from others during this time? Why or why not? Are there certain types of support you feel more comfortable with than others? Why?

_____
_____
_____
_____
_____

After reading this chapter and working through the journaling exercises, you may suspect that you have unresolved grief that is complicating the healing process. My best advice is that you seek out a trained counselor to help you move through your unresolved grief in a safe and effective manner. If you believe that the grief you are experiencing is mostly related to the betrayal, I hope this section on the effects of unresolved grief has impressed upon you the importance of allowing yourself to fully grieve during this time in your life. I can't stress enough that this process cannot be rushed and there are no shortcuts. It's very simple; the only way out is through.

CHAPTER 10

Standard Grief Models

There are two common models pertaining to grief that I would like to discuss in this chapter. The first is the widely known Kübler-Ross Grief Cycle. The well-known "5 stages of grief" are as follows:

- Denial
- Anger
- Bargaining
- Depression (mild)
- Acceptance

Although this model can be useful in the way that it may help us understand and expect some of the experiences we might encounter, I have two issues with it. First, it's somewhat misleading because it seems so linear. In reality, grief looks a lot more like the second illustration on this diagram:

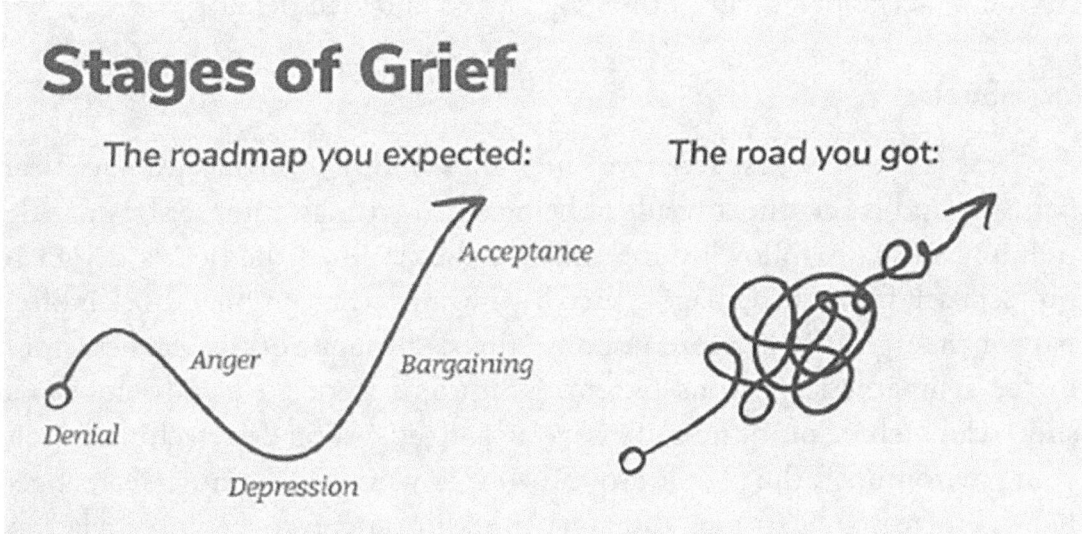

Figure 1: Image taken from SpeakingGrief.org
Copyright© 2020 The Pennsylvania State University

The second issue that I have with the 5-stages model is that it can lead us to be critical of ourselves if we don't fit into these stages, if we don't experience all of the stages, or if we don't progress through them in the way we expect. This can be damaging to our already-broken hearts. As I said earlier in this section, it is important that we give ourselves compassion during this time.

Remember, your grief is uncharted territory and there should be no expectations about how you should feel during the grieving process. The grieving process is as unique as the individual doing the grieving, even though they might be grieving the "same" betrayal or loss. Additionally, if we are going to use this model to look at betrayal grief, there are two extra stages I would like to add that are important to betrayal grief in particular. They are:

- Shock

- Preoccupation

It is important to note that these stages frequently overlap. It's not at all uncommon for partners to be experiencing multiple stages at the same time.

Let's take a look at all of the stages listed above in detail:

Shock

This is the very first stage we enter after finding out that we have been betrayed and is the direct result of being faced with an intense stressor. The numbness usually following the shock is the result of the body's design to protect itself from the damage caused by the impact. Emotional shock is often part of the fight/flight/freeze response that is brought on by the activation of the sympathetic nervous system. Symptoms associated with emotional shock can include numbness, disassociation (the feeling of detachment from your environment, the people around you, or your body), panic, fear, anger, nausea, increased heart rate, difficulty thinking, and even a complete lack of ability to show emotion (a flattened affect). (Boyes, 2018). The initial shock usually wears off relatively quickly, but it typically takes the body 2 weeks to 2 months to come out of this stage. (Stanford).

1. Can you relate to this stage of grief? If so, how? Do you think you're still at this stage? Why or why not?

_____
_____
_____
_____
_____

Denial

This stage can come out in a variety of ways. Examples of denial can be saying things like, "well, at least it's not as bad as so-and-so" or, "at least it wasn't such-and-such". Denial can also take the form of instant forgiveness, premature optimism, or not wanting to know about the important details. The most obvious form of denial is making excuses for your partner, believing implausible reasons for their behavior, or flat-out refusing to acknowledge that there is a problem at all.

1. List any ways that you might be staying in denial of your situation. What are some actions you can take to move through this stage?

_____
_____
_____
_____
_____

Preoccupation

This phase occurs after the reality of the situation sets in. For most wounded partners, this phase is all about making sense of their lives. When you found out about your partner's infidelity, your life shattered into a million pieces. As a result, life as you knew it ceased to exist. This often leaves wounded partners with the feeling that life just does not make sense anymore. The preoccupation phase is all about picking up the shattered pieces and examining them one by one in order to have things make some sort of sense again. It is marked by a preoccupation with the details of the infidelity. Partners often spend all of their free time thinking about the betrayal, analyzing all of the facts, and turning almost every conversation with their partner back to talking about the betrayal. Constantly checking our partners' phones, email accounts, and whereabouts are also common activities associated with this stage. During this time, self-care is more important than ever because of the traumas — both macro and micro — that we experience on a daily (if not hourly) basis when there has been infidelity or betrayal in the relationship. Many partners I work with need a lot of support to get through this.

This phase is crucial to your recovery. That being said, it is important not to hang out here too long. I have had clients come to me that have been checking up on their partners for years, even though they have passed a polygraph, are in recovery, and haven't relapsed into any addictions. In these instances, staying in this phase too long has robbed them of their lives because they can't move forward. Although getting the facts around the betrayal is extremely important, too much time spent here can prevent you from moving forward.

One caveat that I would like to mention here is that it is nearly impossible to get out of this stage if your partner is constantly dribbling out new details and/or is still engaging in their infidelity-related behaviors. We can't move on in the relationship if our partners are not being transparent and are still hiding important information from us.

1. Can you relate to this stage? If so, how? Do you see yourself currently in this stage? If so, how long have you been here?

_____
_____
_____
_____
_____

2. If you answered that you believe that you are in this stage, is it because you keep receiving new information or because you have been fixated on the same information or nuances of the same basic information?

_____
_____
_____
_____
_____

3. Make a list of things that your partner could do to help you not think about the betrayal all of the time and/or ways in which they could act more trustworthily.

_____
_____
_____
_____
_____

Anger

This is the stage that many partners beat themselves up around— often directing their anger inward rather than towards the partner that betrayed them. Societal, personal, and religious expectations around anger can leave us feeling guilty about having angry feelings. Sometimes we put pressure on ourselves to forgive too quickly because we feel bad about being angry. If you feel this way, I would like to tell you that it's not the presence of anger that is problematic, but the way we sometimes behave in our anger that can be problematic. Anger and aggression are natural responses to threat. Both are core components of humankind's survival response. They help us rally ourselves to act in the face of events that are intensely frightening or dangerously out of control. (Blair, 2011). Anger, in particular, is such an important component of our experience as wounded partners that I have devoted separate chapters to the subject later in this book.

How did your family of origin view anger?

_____
_____
_____
_____
_____

Bargaining

Bargaining is a stage typically associated with facing the subject of death. It usually looks like us making promises to God or the universe if our loved one can only be spared. Bargaining in terms of betrayal can look quite different, but it's still usually present in the betrayal grieving process. We may bargain with the pain of betrayal by doing just about anything to avoid the pain of loss. Examples of this could include compromising our own morals and good judgement in order to stay in denial and remain in the past where we perceived that times were better. We also bargain by asking "what if" questions or replaying "if only" scenarios in our minds. We can recognize if we are in the bargaining stage if we keep saying things like, "if only my partner didn't work there, the affair never would have happened". It is our mind's way of refusing to accept the fact that we can't somehow change the fact that partners were unfaithful. Bargaining can even take on the form of guilting or blaming ourselves. This is actually a way that we're attempting to remain in control of an uncontrollable situation. If we can blame ourselves, then the problem lies with us. Guilt and blame may feel bad, but it can also give us a false sense of being able to fix the issue ourselves. If we are the problem and not the other person, then we have the power to fix it all.

1. Do you see yourself bargaining? If so, how are you doing it? What are some ways you can combat doing this in order to move through this phase faster?

_____
_____
_____
_____
_____

Depression (minor)

As I mentioned earlier, major depression is not associated with healthy grief. It is more of a symptom of unresolved grief. (Devan, 1993). However, minor depression in the form of "the blues" or sadness is totally normal and should be expected. After we realize the pain of loss can't be escaped or bargained away, we come to a deep understanding of what we have lost. This often results in sadness and a period of mild depression. Like the preoccupation/fixation stage, partners often need help getting out of this stage. Although feelings of sadness are completely normal, they can trigger a longer-lasting version that may require counseling and even medication. I will also mention that unhealthy coping mechanisms have a way of entering our lives at this stage, so self-care and community are imperative. Addictions and other unhealthy coping mechanisms can keep us stuck here, so be sure to reach out and seek help if you find yourself engaging in any unhealthy behaviors to excess (drinking, smoking, shopping, sleeping, etc.).

1. Have you developed or are you currently engaged in any unhealthy coping mechanisms to deal with your sadness? If so, what are they? List some alternatives to these behaviors.

_____
_____
_____
_____

2. Do you feel that you've been stuck in depression for a prolonged period of time? Are you currently seeking out help for this? If not, list actions you can take to address this issue. Also, list date(s) in the near future you are going to dedicate to addressing this issue.

_____
_____
_____
_____

Acceptance

Considered to be the ultimate goal of the grieving process, most people believe that acceptance is sort of a finish line that means that they are finally done grieving. Although getting to acceptance can improve our outlook on the other stages of grief and on life in general, the idea that we're completely done is misleading. Acceptance doesn't mean that things are suddenly "all better". It means that we have now accepted our losses as part of our new reality, and that we can stop trying to relive the past and now engage fully in our future. We understand that we can't change the past or regain what was lost, but that loss does not have to define our existence and there is plenty of potential for good things to happen moving forward. In this stage, we can start reclaiming our lives. It is important to note that **acceptance does not mean that we consider our partner's actions to be acceptable**. It only means that we accept that whatever happened has happened and we can now concentrate on moving forward from that point. There is a big difference between those two things. Acceptance is centered around acknowledging and accepting our new reality and learning how to function in that new reality in a healthy manner.

1. Are the above-expressed views on what acceptance is and isn't new to you? How can you use this information to help you in your healing journey?

_____
_____
_____
_____
_____

The second model of grief is Worden's Tasks of Mourning developed by psychologist William Worden in his book entitled *Grief Counseling and Grief Therapy: A Handbook for the Mental Health Practitioner*. (Worden, 1991). In his model, Worden outlines four specific tasks that must be accomplished during the grieving process. Although tasks 3 and 4 of the model need to be adjusted in the case of grief associated with betrayal, I personally find this model more useful than the Kubler-Ross model. Also, it is important to note that, much like the "stages of grief", these tasks can overlap and it's not uncommon for partners to be engaged in more than one task at any particular time.

Task 1: To Accept the Reality of the Loss

This task is simple in essence, but not easy to accomplish. One of the biggest hurdles here is that research has shown that our brains are averse to loss. This is amplified when we perceive the "thing" we are losing to be of high value. The higher the perceived value, the harder it is for our brains to accept the loss. (DeMartino, et. al., 2010). As a society, we place a very high value on having a relationship. We place an even higher value on having a "perfect" one. The reality is that no relationship is perfect. However, if we've put a high value on this concept, and even the image of "perfect" is threatened, it makes it hard for our brains to let go and accept the loss.

Another issue that frequently complicates this task is our need to remain in control. Humans dislike being helpless and have a deep-seated desire for certainty and control. The very idea that we are subject to forces greater than ourselves can be terrifying and unsettling. (Leotti, et. al., 2010). In the lesser sense, studies have shown that some control is beneficial to human beings because a sense of competence can boost well-being. (Fotiadis, et. al., 2019). However, studies have also shown that a need to control circumstances outside of our locus of control, or the need to control others, can make us truly miserable and even shorten our lifespans. (Raghunathan, 2016). Unfortunately, betrayal reminds us that we are not always able to remain in control. This is hard for our brains to accept.

Task 2: To Process the Pain of Grief

Again, this task is fairly straightforward. However, it too is not easily accomplished. Much of the struggle lies in the fact that humans have a propensity for seeking out pleasure and avoiding pain. An extreme example of this can be seen in addiction where the addict is both chasing pleasure and avoiding or relieving pain (particularly emotional pain) at the same time. Although the addiction example doesn't apply to most of us, to some extent we all engage in this behavior. This is outlined in Sigmund Freud's Pleasure Principle, — which explains why it can be hard to delay the pleasure of comfort when we are in pain. However, processing the pain of grief is the only way we can avoid setting ourselves up for major problems related to unresolved grief in the future.

Task 3: To Adjust to a World Without the Deceased

Here is the first task of grieving that needs to be adjusted for the grief associated with betrayal. If I had to give a name to this Task as it relates to losses associated with betrayal, I would call it "Adjusting to a World Without Life as We Knew It". In most cases, the person who betrayed us is not deceased. However, losing the bonds connected to that person can be much like a death. Relational bonds hold deep meaning for us. We feel betrayed, disappointed, and utterly dismayed when those meanings are lost. The truth as we knew it has been shattered. Although relationships can be restored, not only must we accept that the relationship as we knew it is gone, but we must also adjust our lives to accommodate that loss. These adjustments can be external (how life has changed), internal (how this has affected us), and spiritual (how this has affected our beliefs or view of God or our overall spirituality).

Task 4: To Find an Enduring Connection with the Deceased While Embarking on a New Life

This is the second task of grieving that needs to be adjusted for betrayal grief. If I had to give a name to this one, I would call it "Grasping Our New Reality and Moving Forward Within That Reality". We have ended up in a situation that, despite our best efforts, we simply can't change. Acceptance of past events and the resulting changes to our lives can be a very powerful tool in helping us to move forward. When we get stuck in the past, we disempower ourselves in that we can't effectively make important decisions about how to move forward. We do not have to want, support, or even like what we are accepting, but we must accept that it has happened just the same. We can use mindfulness to create an active, open attention to the present and work on accepting things as they are. Only then can we begin to move forward in our new reality.

1. Which task(s) do you see yourself currently working on? How are you doing that?

_____
_____
_____
_____
_____

CHAPTER 11

An Unconventional Grief Model and Grieving Tips

I would like to highlight a third possible model for dealing with grief: The Bridges Transitions Model. This model was originally developed to help businesses effectively manage their employees' reactions to change, but I believe it can be applied to betrayal grief also. In his book *Transitions*, Bridges describes 3 stages an individual goes through during the process of change. A concept that is central to this model is the difference between change and transition. According to Bridges, change is external to people and happens to them whether they like it or not. I think that we as wounded partners can all relate to this part, as the changes brought on by the infidelity were thrust upon us and were completely out of our control. Transition, on the other hand, is the internal psychological process that people go through because of change. It is all about how we feel as we come to terms with the changes taking place in our lives. Change can happen very quickly, whereas transition usually takes much longer. As opposed to change which we had no control over, we can embrace the stages of transition as we move toward a new future. (Bridges, 2004).

Much like the stages of grief or the tasks of grieving outlined previously, the stages of transition can coexist at the same time. This is important to realize as wounded partners so that we don't get frustrated with ourselves and feel like we're going backwards. Let's take a closer look at the 3 stages of transition:

The Ending: According to Bridges, all transitions begin with an ending. In the case of betrayal, wounded partners are faced with an ending because life as we understood it is now over. The abrupt changes brought on by infidelity cause many losses and, as we move toward being okay again, we end up letting go of a lot of things. These things could include our outlook on life, beliefs about our partner, hopes and dreams, a feeling of security, emotional safety, and definitely trust. Common feelings during this stage include anger, fear, sadness, frustration, denial, and disorientation.

The Neutral Zone: The next step after The Ending is The Neutral Zone. When I think of this stage, I'm reminded of a quote by Nancy Levin:

"Honor the space between no longer and not yet."

The neutral zone is that space between no longer and not yet. It can be the most uncomfortable stage for wounded partners because they feel stuck and often feel scared. The relationship as they knew it is no longer, but they haven't traveled far enough into the transition to get a clear view of what is up ahead. Although this stage can be highly unpleasant, it is central to the transition process. Here, we as wounded partners are gaining new skills, strength, and insights that will help carry us into the future. According to Susan Bridges, *"The essence of life takes place in the neutral zone phase of transition. It is in that interim spaciousness that all possibilities can come to life and flourish".* During The Neutral Zone stage, the new beginning has actually already begun. We just can't see it yet. This can cause a significant amount of distress. Many of us just want our life back, but we know we are powerless to undo what the wounding partner has done. Common feelings during this stage can include depression, doubt, confusion, uncertainty, resentment, disorientation, and hopelessness. Coping during this stage takes almost all of the wounded partner's energy.

The New Beginning: As opposed to the other two stages that cause disorientation, The New Beginning stage is about reorientation. In this stage, if we have embraced recovery, we have developed new skills, understanding, and attitudes that will propel us forward into a hopeful new phase of life. Instead of mourning what was lost, we evaluate what we have left and move forward with a new understanding and purpose. It is important to realize that, if we are to reach this stage, we need to actively embrace our own recovery instead of avoiding it.

Common experiences and feelings during this stage can include a renewed sense of purpose, hopefulness, empowerment, high energy, and an openness to possibility.

Although Bridges' Transition Model is most often used in a business setting by managers helping employees embrace organizational change, it can be useful to us as wounded partners. It helps provide a framework for what's happening to us internally because of the massive changes taking place in our lives.

1. Do you find Bridges' Transition Model useful for your situation? Why or why not?

2. Where do you see yourself within the 3 stages described above? How do you feel about that?

Tips For Moving Through Grief

I have already mentioned several ways for wounded partners to navigate grief and loss in other parts of this week's lesson. However, I would like to give you some important tips for navigating grief successfully, even if some of those previously mentioned are being reiterated here.

Accept loneliness, but don't let yourself get isolated.

Grief can be a lonely process. Even if we have contact with others that have been betrayed, each situation is unique and almost everyone we talk to will have different circumstances that they are grieving, and different reactions to those circumstances. Also, sometimes we just don't feel like talking to anyone. This is okay and completely normal. However, don't let yourself get isolated. Plan to reach out regularly to safe friends, trained professionals, and other people who can support you during this process.

Don't ignore or avoid it.

Remember, unresolved grief can lead to health problems and other complications. Your best solution to healing the pain of grief is to work through it.

<u>Get some sleep.</u>

This may seem like a no-brainer, but it still needs to be said. If you have ever raised children, you know that when they are tired and cranky they don't react very well to even the most minor of inconveniences and problems. The same holds true for adults. Humans don't do well when they are sleep deprived. A lack of sleep usually makes things worse and can lead to higher stress levels, a heightened sense of frustration, and even depression and anxiety. It can also significantly affect memory, judgement, and overall mood. (Kaufmann, et. al., 2016). Setting a regular sleep schedule and practicing good sleep hygiene (employing a "winding down" ritual, avoiding heavy meals, etc.) can help.

<u>Express and release your emotions.</u>

Giving ourselves the space and self-compassion we need to express our emotions is key to the grieving process. Remember, there is no right or wrong way to feel when we're grieving. Obviously, talking with others is helpful in letting out our feelings, but other activities can be too. Some of these include:

- Writing a letter or journaling
- Listening to music
- Exercising
- Expressing ourselves artistically
- Engaging in other creative activities (baking, building something, taking a class, etc.)

<u>Validate your grief.</u>

A good way to do this is by talking with others who have had or are having similar experiences. Another way is through talking with a trained counselor or coach who can help you understand that what you are feeling is normal. Reading this book will also help you validate your grief.

Help others help you.

Many people want to help those who are grieving but are at a loss as to how. Here are some things you can communicate to others so that they can help you:

- They can give you the space to share your sorrow without commenting.
- They can refrain from offering false comfort or platitudes such as "it was for the best" and "time heals all wounds".
- They can offer practical help such as cooking or babysitting.
- They can show patience.
- They can simply give you a hug from time to time.
- They can refrain from criticizing your partner.
- They can refrain from giving you advice based on what they think that they would do in your situation.

1. Are there any of these areas that you are doing well in? If so, what are they? List any areas in which you need to improve. How can you do that?

_____
_____
_____
_____
_____

Counting Your Losses

As you move forward through the grieving process, it is important to recognize your losses so that you can properly grieve them. Affairs, pornography, and intimacy avoidance create numerous losses for the wounded partner. Some of these could include:

Respect/Admiration for Your Partner	Love for Your Partner
Peace in the Household	Rest/Sleep
Interdependence	Grounding
Appetite	Trust in Yourself
Safety/Security	The Feeling of Being Important
What Your Relationship Was	
Who You Thought Your Partner Was	
The Ability to Laugh	Confidence
Trust in Your Partner	Enjoyment of Sex
Trust in God	Sense of Safety
Trust in Others	Meaning of Your Life
Control of Thoughts and Feelings	Future Plans
Cohesive Family	Self-Respect/Dignity
Ability to be Honest with Others	Friendships
Trust in Reality	Enjoyment of Activities

1. Do you relate to any of the losses? If so, which ones?

_____
_____
_____
_____
_____

2. Are there any losses not on the list that you are currently feeling? If so, what are they?

_____
_____
_____
_____

3. Did you experience any feelings as you made your list of losses? If so, what were they?

_____
_____
_____
_____

4. Were any of these feelings frustrating or uncomfortable for you? Which ones were they?

_____
_____
_____
_____

5. Do you have any particular feeling(s) associated with your losses that you have an urge to avoid? If so, which one(s)? Why do you think you want to avoid it/them?

_____
_____
_____
_____

6. Have you had success grieving losses in the past? If so, what were some of the things you did that helped you work through those losses?

_____
_____
_____
_____

7. Which particular loss(es) do you feel most acutely? Why do you think that is? What is particularly powerful or meaningful about that/those loss(es)?

_____
_____
_____
_____

8. Which loss(es) do you think you might be able to look at differently? Do you think this could be helpful to you? If so, how?

_____
_____
_____
_____

CHAPTER 12

Anger

"Grief's first-born child is anger. She who storms from room to room, windows rattling in her wake, destruction her middle name, and she does not apologize for it. Hurricane in your chest, storm in your soul; she won't release you till you shatter."

-Excerpt from the poem "Children of Grief" by Nikita Gill-

What is Anger?

Anger as a Primary Emotion

Most of us have heard the phrase "anger is a secondary emotion". This holds true in many cases. Anger is a powerful emotion that we feel in reaction to stimuli (either external or internal) that threaten our physical, emotional, psychological, or spiritual wellbeing. When this happens, we often feel fear first and then anger. The anger warns us that something is wrong, and we need to be prepared to respond to danger. For some, anger can be used as a smokescreen to cover up fear, vulnerability, or shame. A person using anger in this way often hopes that the people in their life won't catch on to the fact that they really feel small and helpless. These are two examples of how anger can be a secondary emotion.

That being said, I do not agree that anger is always secondary. As I wrote above, anger is a powerful emotion we feel in response to threat, both internal and external. This makes it similar to other primary emotions. Psychologists agree that fear, joy, disgust, contempt, surprise, and sadness are primary, or basic, emotions, and disagree on whether or not anger should be included in that list. This is because some believe that anger is always a response to other emotions as opposed to outside stimuli. However, in my experience working with wounded partners, and as one myself, anger is often the primary emotion felt to the exclusion of all others.

This is why I have concluded that anger is both a primary and a secondary emotion, depending on the situation. When I coach wounded partners (and let me say that anger is an issue for at least 90 percent of them), I do ask if there is some other feeling underlying the anger and I get back quite a few affirmative responses. However, to assume that a wounded partner's anger is only secondary would be a mistake. If that were my conclusion, I would then have to assume that the anger can be easily and quickly dealt with because it's not the source of the real problem. This would do a disservice to many of my clients. For them, *anger is the single biggest hurdle they have to overcome and the most common place for them to get stuck.* When this happens, anger takes center stage and becomes the primary emotion that they have to deal with. If there are any feelings beneath

the anger (and sometimes there aren't any), they are likely to be discovered at a later date. However, the anger has become so huge that it has taken over and, therefore, must be dealt with on its own.

Compounding the issue of anger is the fact that many wounded partners feel guilt, shame, or fear about their angry feelings. This is especially true of my clients who belong to any of the Abrahamic religions (which include Christianity, Judaism, and Islam). For these individuals, forgiveness is fundamental to their faith, and they often see their anger as standing in the way of their religious duty to forgive. It is not uncommon for these clients to want to skip dealing with anger altogether and jump straight to forgiveness. Although I appreciate their need to forgive, this plan of action never works out very well. Jumping immediately to forgiveness almost always results in repressed anger, which I will be discussing later on in this section.

Regardless of which belief system my clients subscribe to, many often have problems giving themselves permission to feel their anger. It is much easier for many of them to let themselves feel shame, sadness, or anxiety than it is to feel, or even admit to feeling, rage and/or anger. Here are some common reasons people are hesitant to "own" angry feelings:

- Fear of losing the relationship
- Have deemed angry feelings as being "bad" or "wrong"
- Feel like a bad person for being angry
- Fear of being gaslit by their partners or others
- Don't feel worthy to have feelings that conflict with the wishes of their partner
- Fear of hurting others
- Fear of being judged by the wounding partner
- Discomfort with showing emotions in general
- Family of origin didn't support showing anger
- Fear of causing further conflict by expressing anger
- Fear of disappointing God

1. On a scale of 1-10, how angry are you about your partner's infidelity-related behavior? Remember, no one is going to read your answer, so be honest.

_____
_____
_____
_____

2. Could you relate to any of the reasons listed above as to why some people have a hard time owning their angry feelings? If so, which ones?

_____
_____
_____
_____
_____

The Physiology of Anger

As I established earlier, anger is a fundamental response to external and internal stimuli that are perceived as threats. As such, the emotion of anger triggers a fight or flight response from the sympathetic nervous system. When this is triggered, the body undergoes multiple changes in preparation for a physical response to a threat. (Yadav, et. al., 2017). These include:

- Increased breathing rate
- Increased heart rate
- Muscle tension
- Changes to facial coloring (increased redness or paleness)
- Sweating
- Shaking, especially of the hands
- Rise in body temperature

These changes take place because the autonomic nervous system (which the sympathetic nervous system is a part of) floods the body with stress hormones such as adrenaline and cortisol. Additionally, blood flow is redirected from the gut to the muscles, and especially the hands, in preparation for physical exertion in the form of fighting. The arousal caused by all of this is very intense and can take anywhere from several hours to a few days to fully recover from. During this slow cool-down period, a person has a higher-than-normal likelihood of being retriggered and/or responding intensely to even minor triggers. (Hendricks, et. al., 2013). You can see how this could create a problem for the wounded partner who has been traumatized and is getting re-triggered frequently throughout the day. Due to these constant triggers and reminders, a betrayed partner can be thrown into a vicious cycle of anger. This is one of the main explanations of why we can get, and stay, so angry. This leads us to the next section.

Why am I so Angry?

There are a few main reasons why wounded partners feel so angry. The scenario I described above is one of those reasons. Another is that we often feel anger in response to other powerful emotions — and nothing creates powerful emotions quite like infidelity.

When a person discovers that their partner has been unfaithful, anger is pretty much a universal response. The reason for this is because we care, and our heart is broken as a result. This is an example of anger as a secondary emotion. In the case of a broken heart, the primary emotion we're likely to feel is sadness. When a wounded partner shows up angry, here are the most common underlying feelings:

- Fear
- Disgust
- Sadness
- Hurt
- Disappointment
- Jealousy
- Betrayal
- Shame

Most of the feelings listed above don't need an explanation as to why they would lie beneath an angry surface. However, I think that the last one, shame, does require an explanation of how it relates to wounded partners.

You would think that, since we are not the ones who acted shamefully, we wouldn't feel shame. However, in my experience, many of us feel it anyway. For those of us that do, it is typically because we take the actions of our unfaithful partner personally. By this, I mean that we perceive our partner's actions to be a result of some sort of inadequacy, insufficient effort, inferiority, or unworthiness on our part. In other words, wounded partners who feel shame after they are betrayed often attribute their partner's behavior to their own perceived character flaws. An example of this is feeling your partner was unfaithful because you've gained weight, have been fighting with them a lot lately, or have not been able to give them the sex that they say they need. Let me be clear; your partner's infidelity is absolutely NOT your fault, no matter what the circumstances. *Your partner's decision to use infidelity as a way to cope with any type of stressor is 100% their responsibility, not yours.*

The tendency to find fault within oneself is due, in large part, to the human brain's capacity for pattern recognition. Pattern recognition is an adaptive skill that helps humans survive because it supports the ability to not only recognize patterns, but to anticipate what might come next when a pattern is recognized. (DeVille, Lee, 2012). Pattern recognition can help us avoid dangerous situations and costly mistakes because our brains constantly match present perceptions with encoded data from past experiences. Part of that encoded data includes past rejection, failures, and mistakes; along with the shameful feelings that accompanied those. When we suffer emotional pain, our brains are far less accurate with those encoded mental matches than they are with physical pain. As a result, the brain is likely to pattern match with other incidences of rejection from the past that aren't related to the current situation. Feelings of shame often accompany those pattern matches because powerful emotions are part of the memories stored. (Levine, 1997).

As wounded partners, I think it is important for us to understand how the brain works so that we aren't caught off guard when we feel shame. It is imperative that we understand that our partner's infidelity is never our fault, and that shameful feelings are inaccurate and unhelpful when dealing with the situation. My hope is that you will start to fight back when feelings of shame creep in and begin to understand that your partner's choices have nothing to do with perceived failures on your part. There were many different ways that they could have dealt with their feelings other than being unfaithful to you. Their infidelity was their choice, and the responsibility and guilt for their actions rest solely with them.

I would be remiss if I did not add that, sometimes, wounded partners are simply angry just because they are angry. Anger is a normal response to the injustice of infidelity. Your partner deceived you and did you wrong. Your anger is a response to their deception and wrongdoing.

I would also like to add that the anger experienced by wounded partners is very different than the anger felt during the grief cycle associated with death. Although some of the questions around *why* the event had to happen are similar between death and betrayal, that is where I find the similarity ends. The anger associated with betrayal grief is different because, instead of simply being angry that an event happened, we have to look at the person who caused it to happen. Not only was the infidelity avoidable, but now we have to interact with a person who purposely chose to act inappropriately and hurt us in this manner. This causes a completely different level of anger that only forgiveness can dissipate, over much time and with much concentrated effort.

As I established earlier, anger is a normal human response that indicates something is dangerous or threatening. In the case of infidelity, it makes complete sense that a wounded partner would feel angry and there doesn't need to be another reason for them feeling that. As I will discuss in the next section, there's nothing inherently wrong with being angry. It is the way we behave while in a state of anger that is typically the problem.

1. Do you agree that the anger associated with betrayal is different than the anger associated with the grief cycle as it pertains to death? Why or why not?

_____
_____
_____
_____
_____

2. Has your anger been particularly intense since you found out about the infidelity? Why or why not?

_____
_____
_____
_____

3. Do you feel shame as a result of your partner's infidelity? Why or why not?

_____
_____
_____
_____

4. Do you understand that your partner's choice to be unfaithful isn't your fault? Write yourself a note to remind yourself of that.

_____
_____
_____
_____

CHAPTER 13

The Destructive Side of Anger

As I wrote earlier, anger in and of itself isn't a problem. However, what we *do and say* in our anger often creates problems for ourselves and for others. The instinctive expression of anger is to act aggressively, since it is a natural, adaptive response to a threat. However, an aggressive response is far more appropriate in a situation that threatens our life than it is to something that threatens our relationship. Expressing angry feelings as assertiveness (showing confidence that your anger is justified) is much more appropriate for a relationship than aggression is. The problem with aggression in relationships is that aggressive acts and words actually tear down the fabric of a relationship. Assertiveness, on the other hand, makes our needs and boundaries clear without running the risk of hurting someone in the process.

Anger is similar to many other emotions in that it needs to be channeled in order to be productive. However, anger is unlike other emotions in the following ways:

- Anger often accompanies other emotions
- Anger can be a catalyst for change
- Anger begs to be expressed
- Anger can be turned in on ourselves
- Repressed anger takes a toll on our physical health

These reasons that make anger different than other emotions are precisely the reasons why it's imperative that we channel our anger correctly. Let's take a closer look at each of these:

1. **Anger often accompanies other emotions.**

Although we have established the fact that anger can be a primary emotion, many times it's a secondary emotion. For that reason, it is important that we evaluate our anger in order to discover what, if anything, lies beneath it. If we use our anger to cover up our vulnerable emotions, we run the risk of denying ourselves the ability to fully heal from our pain and, as a result, will likely end up hurting ourselves and others. As Richard Rohr once said, *"Pain that is not transformed is transmitted."*

1. Do you suspect that you might have emotions underlying your anger? If so, list them here.

_____
_____
_____
_____
_____

2. **Anger can be a catalyst for change**

Anger tells us that something is wrong. Due to this fact, anger can be a powerful catalyst for change. However, when we yell, belittle, use sarcasm, and lash out with name calling, it can be difficult, if not impossible, for someone to listen to us. If this happens, we run the risk of shutting down communication in the relationship and, as a result, possibly ensuring that our needs go unexpressed and unmet. If we don't take the proper time to cool down until we can communicate our issues assertively (as opposed to angrily), we run the risk of cutting off the potential for change.

1. Have you been communicating angrily or assertively? On the left-hand side of the table, write down examples of your most-used angry statements and then list their assertive counterparts on the right-hand side.

Example: (Angry) "You're being such a jerk!"	Example: (Assertive) "When you do "x", I feel hurt and angry. I need you to stop."

3. Anger begs to be expressed.

For many of us, it can seem like we are going to burst if our anger is not expressed. This is because the presence of anger is an indication that something is wrong and needs to change, resulting in an intense urge to speak up. The intensity of our angry feelings can lead us to speak before we calm down and think, often creating destruction instead of the change we really need.

4. Anger can be turned in on ourselves.

Sigmund Freud, the founder of psychoanalysis, was the one who famously said that "anger turned inward is depression." Research has shown that this is an oversimplification of the mental health issue of depression. (Blease, 2014). However, for some people, unexpressed anger can lead to depression, which is very serious. For others, anger turned inward can result in self-loathing. Negative self-talk and self-loathing can cause us to be paralyzed with self-doubt, which can lead us to pull away from opportunities that would help us grow.

1. Are you angry with yourself or do you blame yourself in any way for your partner's infidelity? Why or why not?

2. Even if you logically know that you shouldn't blame yourself for your partner's choices, are there any signs that you might be subconsciously blaming yourself? If so, what are they?

___

5. Repressed anger can take a toll on our health.

For some wounded partners, especially partners of intimacy avoidants, intimacy anorexics, or sexual anorexics, expressing anger often falls on deaf ears. Or, even worse, we are blamed for our feelings of anger or made to feel that we're overreacting or even crazy. This leads to a situation where we may repress our anger because to express it is futile. Repressed anger often shows itself in the form of sadness, sarcasm, cynicism, defensiveness, and unhealthy coping mechanisms such as overeating, drug and alcohol abuse, etc. (Munhall, 1993). I often see partners who exhibit the following problems stemming from repressed anger:

- Muscle tension and pain
- Digestive issues
- Headaches
- Overweight

- Chronic fatigue
- Sleep issues

If this describes you, I recommend that you see a trained counselor or coach who can help you express your repressed anger and other emotions in healthy ways.

1. Do you think you repress your anger? Why or why not?

___

2. If you answered yes to Question 1, list any physical symptoms that you're currently experiencing that you suspect might be due to repressed anger.

___

3. If unattended, list ways in which you could attend to the physical symptoms listed in Question 2. List how you will accomplish this.

___

Anger as a Weapon

The most common way I see anger being misused is when wounded partners use their anger as a weapon. Typically, this comes in the form of verbal and/or emotional abuse. Ambrose Bierce once said:

"Speak when you are angry, and you will make the best speech you will ever regret."

Boy, was he right. How many of us have said things in the heat of anger and later regretted what we said? Probably all of us at one time or another.

It's important that I preface the next part of this section by saying that I understand that not all of you are in the frame of mind to save your relationship, and that's okay. However, in my experience, that may not be how you always feel. I have attempted to help many wounded partners in their relationships that, at first, didn't want to stay and then later decided to try to make it work. I can tell you that there have been several cases where the damage done by words on the part of the wounded partner was so severe that the wounding partner no longer wanted to participate in the recovery process, and it was too late to do anything about it. I would also like to add that, even if your relationship can't be salvaged, anger is never an excuse for any kind of abuse.

For us as wounded partners, it's important that we keep a check on our tongues because we deal with angry feelings on a daily basis. Due to the onslaught of triggers we face, anger management skills are of the utmost importance. This is especially true in the early days of discovery/disclosure. Attempts to communicate our pain can dissolve very quickly into verbal attacks and even verbal/emotional abuse. I don't write this to put more pressure on you in an already unfair situation. However, much damage can be done in the aftermath of infidelity through the words that we choose to communicate our anger.

Consider the following analogy:

Imagine your relationship like a city in that it contains structures that are built carefully over time. Now, imagine your partner's infidelity as a hurricane that swept through the city of your relationship. The aftermath of this storm is terrible. Almost all of the buildings are torn down and most of the materials used to build those structures have been reduced to rubble. The two or three structures left standing are shaky at best. Now, imagine your anger as a tornado poised to sweep through the broken city of your relationship. Used incorrectly, the tornado can, and will, do further damage to the few structures left standing. If it is allowed to go unchecked, there may be nothing left to salvage after the storm has cleared.

Although there are several things that can further damage a relationship suffering from the aftermath of infidelity, unchecked anger in the form of verbal/emotional abuse is potentially the most toxic and damaging to a relationship that is already on a shaky foundation. Here are some signs that your attempts to communicate your hurt and pain have veered into verbal/emotional abuse territory:

- You insult your partner

- You attempt to verbally (or otherwise) humiliate your partner for their actions

- You ridicule your partner

- You give your partner the silent treatment as a way to punish them

- You yell or scream at your partner

- You shame your partner and/or attack their value as a human being

- You use threats to get them to do what you want

Of course, we all fail in this area sometimes — especially after the discovery or disclosure of infidelity. It is important to understand that we all do these things now and then, and that a few mistakes in this area don't mean the death of your relationship. That being said, don't let the anger over your partner's actions become an excuse to engage in abusive behavior. Even if you don't plan on staying in the relationship, it is important to realize that communicating anger in an abusive way is never okay, regardless of another person's actions.

1. Do you think your anger has become uncontrolled to the point that it could be destructive? Why or why not?

_____
_____
_____
_____
_____

2. If you answered yes to Question 1, in what ways has your anger become destructive; either to others or to yourself?

_____
_____
_____
_____
_____

3. List ways in which you can manage your angry feelings less destructively.

_____
_____
_____
_____
_____

Anger Can Be Harmful to Us Long-Term

"Anger is an acid that can do more harm to the vessel in which it is stored than to anything on which it is poured."

-Mark Twain-

Earlier in this book, you learned that angry feelings often a sympathetic nervous system response. Feelings such as fear, anxiety, and even excitement can also trigger the same response. However, if the thoughts preceding the response were angry in nature, one can assume that the emotion of anger is at the root. Common anger-triggering thoughts tend to center around the following patterns of thinking:

- Personalization (the belief that events are somehow due to our shortcomings or perceived flaws or that someone's bad behavior is due to something we did)

- Overgeneralizing (taking one bad event and applying it to everything)

- Catastrophizing (assuming fears are facts)

- Mind Reading (assuming you know what people are thinking)

- Perfectionism (with ourselves or others)

- Emotional reasoning (thinking a feeling means something about us)

- Labeling (taking a behavior and turning it into the totality of our value or another person's value)

- Mental filtering (taking criticisms as fact but reducing the value of a compliment, or highlighting our virtues and downplaying another person's virtues)

- Unfair comparisons (comparing our worst features to someone's best features, or assuming that someone has it all together and we pale in comparison)

- Black and white (polarized) thinking

- Fallacy of fairness (things should be "fair")

All of the examples above can be described ANTs (automatic negative thoughts), also known as cognitive distortions. A cognitive distortion is a type of distorted thinking that is typically inaccurate, at least in part, and has a heavy negative bias. Although no one cause is noted for the development of cognitive distortions, one thought is that they can develop over time in response to unfavorable events that did harm to an individual. Some common examples of cognitive distortions would be catastrophizing, all-or-nothing thinking, and jumping to conclusions.

Stress is also believed to play a significant role in the development of cognitive distortions. Research suggests that the more prolonged the stress is, the more likely it is for a cognitive distortion to form as a type of adaptation or protection mechanism for an individual's immediate survival. (Frey, Epkins, 2002). Although the idea of negatively biased thinking as a coping mechanism may sound strange, it makes perfect sense because, if a person regularly expects adversity, they may be better equipped to handle it when it comes. The issue with adapting in this way is that, over time, it becomes maladaptive. The individual who thinks this way may actually be responsible for repeated negative events in the form of self-fulfilling prophecies.

Many of us may already be dealing with cognitive distortions that were formed around negative interactions in our past. For others, the threat of developing cognitive distortions is a real one. For wounded partners dealing with the prolonged stress of infidelity, distorted thinking becomes a likely threat in response to the negative events unfolding in their lives. This is another reason why dealing with anger correctly is so important. If left unchecked, angry feelings can create a vicious cycle and, over time, can create distorted thinking that lasts a lifetime. This is unfortunate because it can keep us from having what we want out of life, whether we move on from the relationship with our wounding partner or not. The tricky thing about cognitive distortions is that they feel true.

The truth about our circumstances is that they don't cause our emotions. Rather, it is our interpretation of an event that causes us to feel certain emotions. For example, if we get angry that we didn't get a promotion, it is likely that the fact that we didn't get the promotion means something to us. Perhaps we think that we are stupid because we feel embarrassed for not getting the promotion (emotional reasoning), we are a loser (personalization of events), we are never going to get a good job (overgeneralization), or that nothing good will ever happens to us (catastrophizing). As you can imagine, thoughts associated with these statements can leave us with feelings of hopelessness, anger, low self-worth, frustration, and even self-righteousness. These are just a few examples of how cognitive distortions can affect our emotions. You can change the way you feel by changing the way you think. The first step is to recognize when your thinking is related to a cognitive distortion. When we recognize cognitive distortions, we can begin to gain power over them.

1. Do you think you might be dealing with negative patterns in thinking from your past? Why or why not? If so, how do you think these cognitive distortions might be coloring how you view your current situation?

___

___

___

___

___

2. Do you recognize any ways that you might be thinking about your current situation that could be related to cognitive distortions? If so, what are those?

___

___

___

___

___

The next step to overcoming cognitive distortion is to understand what kind of benefit you might be getting from thinking that way. The benefits we get from distorted thinking are called secondary gains. Here are some common secondary gains to distorted thinking:

- Sense of control
- Protection
- Avoidance
- Comfort

1. For the cognitive distortions listed above, list the benefits you may be getting from these.

_____
_____
_____
_____
_____

Next, is to understand how your distorted thinking is actually undermining you. For example, it may feel safe to expect the worst, but in reality it could be keeping you from trying new things that could benefit you. Here are some negative impacts of cognitive distortions:

- Increased anxiety
- Increased depression
- Relationship difficulties
- Health problems
- Emotional distress
- Keep us stuck

1. For the cognitive distortions listed above, list ways that distorted thinking could be negatively affecting you.

_____
_____
_____
_____
_____

The final step to overcoming cognitive distortions is to challenge the thoughts when they present themselves. Here are some ways we can challenge our distorted thinking:

- Reframe the situation

- Imagine other positive scenarios

- Ask yourself if your thoughts are based on feeling or fact

- Consider the evidence (what evidence is there that your thoughts are not completely correct?)

- Weigh the pros and cons of your thinking

1. Select at least one of the cognitive distortions listed above. In one column, write your thoughts around the situation. In the second column, list any evidence you can think of that might tell you why your thinking may not be completely correct. In the third column, list another way you could see the situation that might be more helpful to you.

Here is an example of the type of exercise that I have personally used and has helped me in my own recovery journey:

My negative/unhelpful thought	Is this completely true?	How do I feel when I think this?	When I think this, I want to…	What evidence do I have that this though isn't true?	What would I tell someone I loved if they had this thought?	A more helpful thought is…

CHAPTER 14

Using Anger to Your Advantage

Anger Can Be Helpful

For many of the reasons stated above, anger often gets a bad rap. However, anger can be useful as well. Remember, it isn't having angry feelings that is the problem; it is how we behave in our anger that can be problematic.

We have already covered the fact that anger, when used correctly, can be a powerful catalyst for change. Here are some ways in which anger can help you drive change:

- It can help you get your needs met
- It can help you discover your boundaries
- It can help you get things done
- It can help strengthen your relationships

Let's take a look at these in closer detail:

1. Anger can help you get your needs met.

Remember when we discussed that anger is a signal that something is wrong? When you feel anger, listen to your gut because it's telling you that you might have an unmet need. Unfortunately, in the case of infidelity, the need that you had for your partner to be faithful to you is the one that initially went unmet. However, your anger around new events can help you identify what your needs are moving forward.

2. Anger can help you discover your boundaries.

Again, it is unfortunate and unacceptable that your boundary around being in a relationship with rules regarding infidelity-related behavior was crossed. However, your anger can be a catalyst for new boundaries moving forward. Your anger around the situation can give you the energy you need to delineate what you will and will not accept in the future.

3. Anger can help you get things done.

While anger can give you the energy to set new boundaries, it can also help you to enforce those boundaries moving forward. If your partner crosses a boundary that you have in place or is acting in ways that feel unsafe, anger will typically be your first clue that something's wrong. Listen to your gut and use your anger to act when needed.

4. Anger can strengthen your relationships.

For some, conflict is a thing to be avoided. For others, it's the misuse of anger that weakens their relationships. When we are angry, conflict is typically the result. However, handled correctly, conflict can lead to a clearer understanding of where we stand in our relationships, as well as where other people stand. When we are afraid of making others angry or of our own anger, we don't act and that can lead to repressed anger. When we abuse others with our words or actions because we are angry, we run the risk of driving distance between us and them. It is when we express our anger, in the form of assertiveness, within the confines of love, that we can be heard without hurting ourselves and others.

1. List ways in which you can see your anger could be helpful to you.

_____
_____
_____
_____
_____

Anger Management

"If you are patient in one moment of anger, you will escape a hundred days of sorrow."

-Chinese Proverb-

Since how we act in our anger tends to create so many problems for human beings in general, there is a lot of information out there regarding anger management. With wounded partners, I find the following techniques to be the most helpful:

- The practice of self-regulation
- Time-outs
- Anger work
- Self-care
- Willing Hands
- Trigger plans

Let's take a look at each of these in further detail:

1. The Practice of Self-Regulation

In Section 1, I explained that there are things we can do in our everyday lives to help engage the parasympathetic nervous system and calm down the sympathetic nervous system. Since I have already established that angry feelings often trigger a fight or flight response from the sympathetic nervous system, it stands to reason that self-regulation in the form of Somatic Experiencing exercises is helpful in managing anger. The best way to practice Somatic Experiencing exercises is to do them throughout the day, every day. Regular practice of self-regulating exercises like these will engage the parasympathetic nervous system and reduce trigger responses over time.

2. Time-Outs

I have established that suppressing anger on a regular basis can do us more harm than good. However, taking a step back to regroup when we're angry can help prevent us from acting in harmful and inappropriate ways. Time-outs are essential for wounded partners because of the emotional flooding that happens when we get triggered. The idea of taking a time-out when triggered is to help get your sympathetic nervous system to calm down enough to have a constructive conversation as opposed to a destructive one. I would like to stress that time-outs, when used properly, should help reduce destructive fighting and enhance communication between partners. You will know if you're using time-outs improperly if your motives are to punish your partner by using the silent treatment or to threaten abandonment.

Time-Out Protocol

- Either partner can call a time-out

- A verbal or non-verbal signal for the need for time-out should be established beforehand

- The request for time-out should be honored. One partner should not follow the other around trying to get them to reengage.

- The conversation needs to stop when time-out is called. No attempting to have the last word.

- Both parties agree that the conversation can resume in 20-30 minutes.

- Both parties should do something calming and constructive during the 20-30-minute time-out. Time-outs don't work if the time is used to sit around and think about what you're going to say next in an effort to win the argument. Focusing on how angry you feel at the other person won't work and might actually make things worse. The idea is to take your mind completely off the argument in order to give your flooded system a break. Appropriate activities to do while on a time-out include reading a book, taking a brisk walk, or taking a bath. These activities, among others, will give your sympathetic nervous system a chance to calm down.

• When you come back from time-out, each partner needs to state two things they appreciate about their mate before resuming the conversation.

• Use "I" statements when communicating your feelings. This doesn't include the statement "I feel that you…." This type of statement is actually an accusation and will most likely be felt by the other person as an attack.

3. Anger Work

Sometimes we do just need to let it all out. However, it is inappropriate to let it out all over other people, including our mate. In cases like this, where the anger is overwhelming, I recommend using this technique adapted from a technique developed by Dr. Doug Weiss:

• Write an anger letter to your mate. Don't hold back. However, keep in mind that they should never read it and it should be destroyed afterward.

• Buy a foam bat or child's wiffleball bat

• Stack a pile of pillows on your bed so that they are above waist level

• Ensure that you are out of earshot of your mate and/or your children

• Read your letter out loud

• Pound away on the pile of pillows saying whatever comes to your mind. Do this until you feel exhausted. If you need to pause, take a break. However, if you still feel anxious or angry, then you need to keeping pounding away until all of it is gone.

• Repeat as necessary

I do a lot of anger work with my clients during individual sessions. Although not all of them are comfortable expressing their angry feelings, most of them tell me afterwards that it was helpful to them.

4. Self-Care

"Self-care is not self-indulgence; it is self-preservation."
-Audre Lorde-

This idea was covered in Section 3, but it bears repeating. There is never a time that is more important for us to practice self-care than when we're dealing with the intense emotions associated with infidelity. Angry feelings can take a toll on our energy, both emotionally and physically. It is important to find ways in which we can fill our empty tanks. Remember, self-care means taking care of ourselves in every area, not just physically. Good self-care includes the physical, spiritual, emotional/mental, social, and financial aspects of our lives. It also involves engaging in active recovery. Refer to your answers in Section 3 to help remind yourself how you plan to take care of yourself.

5. Willing Hands

This exercise comes from Dialectical Behavior Therapy (DBT), which was designed by Dr. Marsha Linehan to help treat personality disorders such as Borderline Personality Disorder. This particular exercise, although very simple, is very effective when a person is dealing with anger. It is based on the idea of acceptance, which is a process by which we can reduce our suffering while increasing our feelings of freedom. Here are the simple instructions for the Willing Hands exercise:

- Sit with your eyes closed and imagine a conflict you are facing, and the angry feelings associated with it.

- Sit with that scenario until the feelings of anger have noticeably returned.

- Move your hands into your lap so that they are resting on your knees.

- Open your hands and place them on your knees with your palms upturned toward the sky/ceiling.

Did you feel your anger reduce? When my clients do this exercise, most of them tell me that their feelings of anger reduce as soon as they turn their palms upward. When I do Willing Hands, I always take a deep breath in through my nose and out through my mouth and speak the words, "I accept" while holding my hands in the upturned position. When the words "I accept" are spoken, it doesn't mean that we are saying that the actions of the person we are having conflict with are acceptable. Instead, we are simply accepting the situation as it is and are not fighting against the reality of it. For me, it is also about acknowledging any impulsive or destructive behaviors that I am engaging in around my feelings of anger and letting those go.

6. Trigger Plan

See the following chapter.

CHAPTER 15

Triggers and Reminders

Triggers and reminders are a normal part of the recovery process. A frustrating and painful part of recovery, but a normal part, nonetheless. They are simply a part of dealing with trauma. Because of the way our brains encode information, triggers and reminders can come in the form of obviously similar situations, slight resemblances, poor choices in wording on the wounding partner's part, holidays, or even seasonal changes. There is no limit to how, when, where, and why a trigger or reminder can pop up. Journaling around your triggers and/or doing an exercise like the Trigger Plan below, can help you recognize patterns that will allow you to be more strategic when dealing with a large percentage of your personal triggers and reminders.

It's not uncommon for partners dealing with betrayal trauma to experience dozens of triggers per day in the weeks and months following disclosure. If the disclosure has been "dribbled" out over time, each instance of new information has likely caused a separate trauma for you. This is why I recommend that the wounding partner be 100% upfront and honest during the disclosure process. However, even if they weren't, there is still much hope for you to reduce your triggers and reminders and successfully deal with the ones that persist.

Triggers, reminders, flashbacks, and the like kick our sympathetic nervous system into high gear. As I have already established, this part of our system is responsible for survival. Thus, the fight or flight response is put into effect. Triggers set the brain on high alert and send signals to the body that there is imminent danger that must be avoided. Depending on the personality of the triggered person, they may go on the attack, physically leave, or "check out" emotionally.

Trigger Plan

A method that can be helpful for managing anger, triggers, and reminders of the betrayal is to preemptively do everything we can to avoid escalation once we experience a trigger. Creating a plan for how to deal with triggers is a crucial way for us to manage the onslaught of emotions caused by infidelity. Our partners can help us establish a plan for when we are triggered into the fight or flight response. Here's some information on how to create a solid trigger plan:

Strategy for Dealing with Triggers

At a calm time, establish a plan for when triggers come. It is important to do this at a time when the waters are calm and not in the heat of the moment. This can be somewhat counterintuitive because, when things are going well, the subject of infidelity is not exactly what you want to be talking about. However, this exercise requires rational thought, which is impossible when the sympathetic nervous system is triggering you into fight or flight mode.

While making your plan, your partner can ask you questions like:

1. What would help you feel safe when you are triggered?

2. What can I do?

3. Can you help me understand what is going on with you?

4. What do I do that makes you feel unsafe during these times?

The answers to these and other questions will help you develop your plan. Please note that the plan should be considered an official agreement between you and your partner. It must be adhered to in order to work.

*If you plan to do this exercise as a couple, here is a note to the *wounding* partner: going off script, defending, walling off, or leaving will only serve to escalate the situation and re-wound your partner.

Mapping Your Triggers

For many of us, some work needs to be done around mapping the occurrence of our triggers before we can hope to identify and/or understand them. For this exercise, you are going to need to keep a "trigger mapping journal" in order to record information regarding when and how your triggers happen. Here are the questions you want to answer around "who, what, where, when, and how" each time you notice that you were triggered:

- Where was I?
- What time of day was it?
- How did it happen?
- When did it happen?
- Why do I think it happened?

As you keep a journal, you will begin to see patterns emerging. Once you see a pattern, this will help you identify specifically what the trigger is associated with that pattern. For example, you may notice that you are triggered in a certain type of place. This knowledge will then help you investigate further to find out what the trigger is really about. Although many triggers are obvious and can be added to the "Identifying Triggers" exercise below right away, some triggers may be harder to identify. Keeping an exercise journal will help you do that.

Identifying Triggers

Specific Triggers	How does this apply to your situation?	Action plan
Seeing attractive people (with or without partner)		Hold your partner's hand if in public Tell yourself that you are enough
Sex scenes in movies + TV		Change the channel Research programs before watching
Inconsistency/unreliability of partner (e.g., being late)		Express concerns to partner gently
Times of day Days of the week (e.g., weekends, late nights)		Plan ahead to do something relaxing
Other:		
Other:		
Other:		

Trigger Coping Plan for Couples

The main triggers in our relationship are:	
Strategies for managing triggers:	
Time-out / alone time	
Making a request (e.g., for a hug, reassurance)	
Talking about it (using "I" statements)	
Behaviors to avoid:	

If your relationship has ended or if you are currently separated from your partner and not communicating with them, you are still likely dealing with triggers and reminders. My best advice for you is to develop a plan around self-care and self-regulation for when you get triggered. If you are still in your current relationship, it may be helpful for you to develop an individual trigger plan in addition to your couple trigger plan.

Trigger Coping Plan for Individuals

The main triggers for me are:	
Strategies for managing my triggers:	
Time-out / alone time (list times and days here)	

Using self-regulation techniques (list favorites here)	
Talking about it with a friend, counselor, or coach (List who here)	
Behaviors to avoid: *Situations, people, and conversations to avoid:*	

CHAPTER 16

Loss of Confidence and Self-Worth

I want to begin this chapter by stating that not all partners struggle with this issue as a result of betrayal. It has been my experience that each partner is unique with their own circumstances and background that contribute to their particular reactions and feelings. That being said, I find that roughly 40% of wounded partners struggle, at least in some way, with a loss of self-worth, or at least self-confidence, after betrayal has been discovered. While writing this book, I felt that this percentage was high enough to warrant addressing the subject.

There are many ways in which a wounded partner's confidence and/or self-worth can be lowered after discovery or disclosure of infidelity, and a fair percentage of those are based on comparison to others and/or judgement of ourselves. Thoughts centered around what we could have done better are normal after experiencing betrayal. Painful thoughts and/or comparisons around body image and overall attractiveness are normal as well. This is especially true with sexual betrayal because it involves a person or people that we can directly compare ourselves to. Due to the way our brains are wired for pattern recognition, the recall of past events in which we were betrayed or rejected is also common. These recalls are especially painful if we take on the past rejection or betrayal as somehow our fault. I have had some wounded partners tell me that they also suddenly questioned how interesting or intelligent they were as well.

Partners with existing issues around self-worth are hit especially hard because the betrayal seems to confirm fears that they already had around not being "good enough" in one way or another. Partners of addicts, intimacy avoidants, sexual anorexics, and intimacy anorexics are highly likely to be blamed by their partner for the infidelity-related behavior. This is due to the fact that the shame levels are particularly high in individuals struggling with these issues. The shame prevents them from being willing, or even able, to look at themselves as being the wrong one, and blame is frequently the tool they use to get the focus off of themselves and onto their partner. This tactic, originally coined by psychology researcher Jennifer Freyd, is commonly referred to as DARVO, which stands for "deny, attack, reverse victim to offender". By blaming their partner, the wounding partner can attempt to deny that they are at fault for their wrongdoing because they were "simply reacting as a victim to their partner's behavior". If the partner agrees to take on even a little bit of the responsibility, all the better for them. Even if your partner is not an addict or anorexic, it isn't uncommon for an unfaithful partner to blame their mate, at least initially, in an attempt to get out of looking at themselves and their behavior. In any case, being blamed for someone's infidelity is intensely painful and can be extremely damaging to the one being blamed. Before I continue, let me just reiterate that **your partner's infidelity has nothing to do with who you are and everything to do with who they are. Their choice to be unfaithful is 100% their responsibility.**

Here are some common ways that the self-worth and/or self-confidence of partners get shaken after disclosure or discovery of infidelity:

- Feel isolated, alone, and somehow defective and/or deficient
- Feel embarrassed because they think other people are judging or will judge them
- Compare themselves to an affair partner and/or pornography
- Become afraid to take risks
- Fall victim to an overactive inner critic

I would like to take a closer look at each one of these, as well as provide ways in which you can combat these common issues:

1. Feeling like you are alone and/or are deficient in some way

It's not at all uncommon for wounded partners to feel isolated and alone after the discovery or disclosure of infidelity. However, statistics show that it would be more difficult to find someone who hasn't been betrayed than someone who has. Studies have shown that infidelity is not always a symptom of an unhappy relationship, and that people seek sexual gratification outside of their primary relationships for numerous reasons…most of which have nothing to do with their partners.

2. Feeling like people will judge you or are judging you

There is a lot of truth to the saying, "people are so busy thinking about themselves that they don't have time to think about you." That being said, people can be judgmental and there's no way around that. Keep in mind that just because someone acts judgmentally toward you doesn't mean you have to accept their opinion as truth. Chances are that they are acting that way out of their own insecurities. The best thing you can do is surround yourself with supportive people who understand what you have experienced and treat you lovingly and respectfully. As I established above, it would be harder to find someone who hasn't been betrayed than someone who has. There are many people out there that know exactly how you feel and won't act judgmentally toward you.

3. Comparing yourself to an affair partner or pornography

"No one can make you feel inferior without your consent"
-Eleanor Roosevelt-

Comparing yourself to an affair partner or pornographic images will likely leave you with feelings of inadequacy and frustration. Comparing ourselves to others is not only unkind to ourselves; it allows others to drive our thoughts and behaviors. Because we are acutely aware of our own flaws, we tend to compare ourselves to others unfairly. When we compare someone's features to our own, we put ourselves at a disadvantage and the feelings generated from these unfair comparisons can lead us down a self-destructive path. This includes, for many wounded partners, contacting the affair partner, which, in almost all cases, is NOT recommended. It isn't helpful for several reasons:

- It gives the affair partner more significance than they should have

- Affairs and committed relationships have little in common, so it's an inaccurate comparison

- Affair partners can, and often will, lie and/or manipulate the situation

- They aren't very likely to understand that they have hurt you and if they do, they are unlikely to care

- It will likely create more contact between your mate and the affair partner

- The affair partner won't be able to shed any light on the real reasons behind your partner's actions

I would like to add here that I realize that many of you have already made this mistake. However, if you are considering contacting an affair partner but haven't already, I would ask you to reconsider based on the reasons outlined above. In my experience as a coach, it ends up causing the wounded partner more pain than they are already experiencing.

4. Becoming afraid to take risks

The pain and insecurity felt by wounded partners can result in the development of fear around taking risks. I am not referring to being reckless, like jumping in with both feet after someone has proven themselves unfaithful. However, if you develop a fear around ever taking a chance again on anything, you are likely to hold yourself back from important and meaningful growth opportunities. Early on in recovery, taking a risk could be as simple as finding someone you can trust to talk about the pain with or joining a support group with others who have gone through similar things as you have. Later in recovery, risk-taking could take the form of building a new skill, going back to school, or taking up a hobby that you have always wanted to. It is important that you don't shut yourself off from the world so much that you miss out on ways to help yourself heal.

5. Falling victim to the inner critic

Unfortunately, most of us have an inner critic. However, for wounded partners, the inner critic can become overactive and end up kicking us repeatedly when we are at our lowest. More on the inner critic in the next section.

1. Do you feel that your self-worth and/or self-confidence has been affected by your partner's infidelity? Why or why not?

_____
_____
_____
_____
_____

2. If you answered yes to Question #1, in what ways do you think your self-worth and/or self-confidence has been affected?

_____
_____
_____
_____
_____

What is the Inner Critic?

The term "inner critic" is often used by psychologists to describe the critical inner voice that most of us have that harshly judges or even degrades us. We can tell when we are dealing with the inner critic when our thoughts about ourselves produce feelings of shame, depression, or inadequacy. To help you better recognize if you are dealing with your inner critic, here is a list of inner critic features:

- **It is overly harsh**. If this voice is saying things to you that you wouldn't say to another person, you are dealing with the inner critic.

- **You don't feel in control of it**. A common feeling when dealing with the inner critic is that your thinking has been invaded by a force that you don't recognize or want there.

- **It's repetitive**. When the same negative, demeaning thoughts are playing over and over in your mind, you're dealing with the inner critic.

- **It tends to speak out of context**. If you keep having thoughts around something you've done or said that don't take related incidents into consideration, it's your inner critic speaking.

- **It attacks you for your insecurities**. Even though the inner critic is harsh and critical, which can lead us to feelings of insecurity, it often blames us for being weak and insecure.

- **Its voice often sounds like someone else's**. We all have people in our lives, past or present, who have spoken to us in ways that made us feel shame. The inner critic tends to sound more like these people's voices than our own.

- **It reminds you of your failures**. The inner critic loves to remind us of past failures and missteps. This can leave us paralyzed and afraid to take risks that could lead to personal growth.

- **It tells you you're not good enough**. If there is a voice in your head that tells you ways in which you don't measure up, you are dealing with the inner critic.

- **It makes the idea of self-improvement feel like a heavy weight**. Because the inner critic tells you you're not good enough as you are, thinking of improving yourself can be painful because it feels like you have to self-improve to make up for being deficient to begin with.

- **It won't allow you to accept compliments**. The inner critic's job is to make you feel like you don't measure up. This makes it hard to see the good others see in you and even harder to accept their words of affirmation.

- **It makes you susceptible to the harshness of others.** Since the inner critic already has you feeling bad, it's not a huge leap to take on others' negative opinions about you.

- **It undermines your relationships.** The inner critic attacks us in areas where we already feel insecure. This can deepen feelings of insecurity that can carry over into multiple areas of our important relationships.

1. Do you recognize any ways that your inner critic may be affecting how you think about yourself? If so, what are these ways?

_____
_____
_____
_____
_____

2. List the most common statements your inner critic makes to you on the left-hand side of the table below. On the right-hand side, list positive counter statements to the negative statements. If you need to, ask someone who loves you for help.

Ways Betrayal and the Inner Critic Interact

As I have already established, the inner critic tends to attack us at our most vulnerable points; and nothing creates vulnerability quite like infidelity. Betrayal brings up a host of intense emotions, and we often feel exposed and vulnerable as a result. As we struggle to get a handle on the onslaught of unpleasant emotions, we may act in ways that seem unlike us and even in ways that we aren't particularly proud of. We frequently feel unsafe in sharing our emotions with anyone, in particular the partner who wounded us. It is already hard enough to talk about our feelings around rejection, abandonment, self-worth, and deepest fears. Admitting our innermost feelings around these subjects to the person who betrayed us can make us feel exposed in ways that we haven't experienced before, which can lead us to pull back, withdraw, and even isolate ourselves. The tug-of-war inside of us regarding our emotional vulnerability can cause extreme anxiety, which can cause us to be prone to emotional outbursts in the form of yelling, cursing, crying, or saying things that we don't mean to say.

Enter the inner critic. As I established earlier, the inner critic tends to speak out of context. If we are acting in ways that we aren't particularly proud of or ways we don't understand, our inner critic is often only too happy to speak up and chastise us for being out of control. Of course, this is completely without context. Our inner critic tends to tell us that we should never do certain things, regardless of the circumstances and, when we do, it criticizes us harshly. The inner critic isn't willing or able to give us a break when we most need it.

Another common way in which betrayal and the inner critic interact is around the comparisons we make between ourselves and other people. When we find out our partners have been unfaithful, it is natural to wonder what the other person or people have that we don't have. When the inner critic steps in and reminds us of all of the ways in which we imagine that we are deficient, this can be extremely damaging to our self-worth and/or self-confidence. Instead of the insecure thoughts coming into our heads and passing back out, the inner critic often grabs a hold of them and uses the circumstances of the infidelity to tell us why all of the negative thoughts we have about ourselves are now confirmed.

1. Have you noticed that the voice of your inner critic has gotten louder since you learned of your partner's infidelity? If yes, in what ways has this happened?

_____
_____
_____
_____
_____

2. If you answered "yes" to the question above, in what ways do you think this has affected you?

_____
_____
_____
_____
_____

Ways to Manage the Inner Critic

If your inner critic is out of control, you may need help managing it. If this describes you, there are three therapies that are particularly helpful to people dealing with negative thoughts:

- **Acceptance and Commitment Therapy**: Acceptance and Commitment Therapy (ACT) is an evidence-based therapy that uses acceptance and mindfulness strategies to help a person stay focused on the present moment and to accept thoughts and feelings without judgment. It helps by teaching a person how to work through difficult emotions by focusing on healing instead of dwelling on the negative.

- **Cognitive Behavioral Therapy**: Cognitive Behavioral Therapy (CBT) is an evidence-based therapy that is particularly useful with mood disorders like depression and anxiety but can be used to help with a wide variety of issues. It is a time-limited and structured approach aimed at helping people find new ways to behave by changing their thought patterns.

- **Internal Family Systems Therapy**: Internal Family Systems Therapy (IFS) is an evidence-based therapy that identifies and addresses sub-personalities within a person's greater personality. The greater personality along with sub-personalities make up the individual's internal family system. Some of the sub-personalities represent a person's wounded parts and intense emotions, while others represent parts that try to protect the individual from the pain experienced by their wounded parts. The inner critic would most likely be one of these protective parts.

For those of you who don't feel the need for therapy, here are some tips to help reduce the impact of your inner critic:

- **Name Your Inner Critic**: Give your inner critic a name and acknowledge it when it shows up. Tell it "thank you (name) for showing up, but you are not needed in this situation. I'll take it from here."

- **Practice Self-Kindness**: When your inner critic shows up, take a deep breath before you buy into what it's saying. Practice showing yourself the same kindness that you would show someone else in your situation. Use empathy to combat the inner critic's judgmental statements.

- **Concentrate on Repetitive Movement**: Any repetitive motion that you find calming can help you clear your mind and combat the inner critic. When accompanied by deep breathing, movements such as rubbing two fingers slowly together, rubbing your palms slowly together, rubbing your arm up and down slowly, or even rubbing your earlobe between your pointer finger and your thumb can help you take focus off of your inner critic's negativity.

- **Start a Gratitude Journal:** The Persian poet Rumi once wrote, "Wear gratitude like a cloak and it will feed every corner of your life." Journaling daily about the things you are grateful for (especially about yourself) can help combat your inner critic's negative voice.

- **Develop Awareness Around When it Appears:** Although the inner critic can show up any time, there are often specific places, times, and people that trigger it. Identifying times and situations when your inner critic is likely to appear can help you develop strategies around combatting it.

- **Use Humor:** It may sound ridiculous but giving your inner critic a cartoonish or silly voice can help reduce the weight of its statements.

- **Befriend it.** Often, the inner critic is trying to protect us from experiencing negative events and feelings. Discover what your inner critic is doing for you, thank it, and ask it to move aside so that you can deal with the tough feelings underneath.

CHAPTER 17

Fear

What is Fear?

Fear is a natural human emotion that we feel in response to danger,; either real or imagined. It results from a biochemical response that is universal to every human being along with an emotional response that is unique to every individual. It alerts us to the presence of physical or psychological danger. We fear because it is a basic emotion necessary to the survival of the human race.

Our biological response to fear starts in the amygdala; a part of the brain that is primarily responsible for processing strong emotions. The amygdala has connections to many other brain structures. Thus, it can link to these other areas in order to process both "higher" cognitive functions like reasoning and learning and "lower" functions such as breathing and blood flow. The amygdala is most commonly associated with the fight or flight response I described in previous sections. Once the amygdala sends a distress signal, the hypothalamus activates the sympathetic nervous system. This then sends signals through the autonomic nerves to the adrenal glands, which then pump adrenaline throughout the bloodstream in preparation for fight or flight. As discussed earlier, once the fight or flight response is activated. it can cause us to act in ways that may be viewed as irrational, illogical, and overreactive because our higher cognitive functions are hijacked by the sympathetic nervous system. The amygdala's connection to the parts of the brain that control lower brain functions also explains why we tend to breathe rapidly and get red in the face when we are triggered.

As I wrote previously, our emotional response to fear is as unique as we are. This is because we all have different experiences in our backgrounds that we have attached previous meanings to. For example, I have a friend who is terrified of all dogs because she was bitten by a dog when she was young and concluded (put a meaning in place) that all dogs are dangerous. I, on the other hand, was also bitten by a dog when I was young. However, my family always had dogs while I was growing up and my experience told me that they were friendly. Therefore, I concluded that although the specific dog that bit me was mean, not all dogs were mean. As a result, I'm not terrified of dogs. You can see from this example how two people can experience the same basic event, yet, because of their unique beliefs, can interpret the meaning of that event quite differently. My friend's sympathetic nervous system is activated when she sees a dog, while mine is not.

When I work with wounded partners, and also in my own personal experience, the emotional reaction to the initial fear felt upon discovery of infidelity is at the heart of what we have to recover from. While our partner's behavior was the fear-triggering event that put our bodies and minds into "fight or flight" mode, the resulting landslide of intense emotions in response to that discovery is why it can take us so long to sort the event out for ourselves. Here are some common emotions that tend to follow the primary emotion of fear:

Worry	Desperation	Nervousness
Anxiousness	Doubt	Panic
Horror	Confusion	Shame
Anger	Rage	Repulsion
Guilt		

As you can see, many of the feelings most commonly associated with fear are equally as intense as the fear itself. This is why it can take so long to unwind our thoughts after the discovery of our partner's infidelity. Of course, we can also feel any of these feelings by themselves. However, when we experience these feelings as a result of underlying fear, unwinding them can get complicated.

1. List the fears you have experienced since discovering your partner's infidelity-related behavior.

_____
_____
_____
_____
_____

Common Fears

When we learn about our partner's infidelity, intense feelings such as fear, anger, and sadness are common reactions. One of the reasons that fear is so prevalent among wounded partners is that our partner's unfaithfulness taps into several areas that human beings tend to feel fear around. Let's take a look at each one:

1. **Fear of Rejection**: The fear of rejection is common among human beings as a whole. It is also a fear that many of us face upon discovery of our partner's infidelity. Whether our unfaithful partner's actions signify that they are truly rejecting us or not, infidelity often feels like the worst kind of rejection we have ever experienced. The complicating factors of intimacy avoidance, intimacy anorexia®, and sexual anorexia amplify the issue of rejection because these issues can cause our partner to reject us in both small and big ways on a regular basis. Additionally, if the fear of rejection wasn't there prior to our partner's infidelity, their unfaithful actions can set us up for developing a fear of rejection in the future.

2. **Fear of Inadequacy:** The fear of inadequacy is another common fear that many of us share. Although this fear often stems from issues such as low self-worth and/or self-confidence, our partner's infidelity-related behavior is enough on its own to create a fear of inadequacy. When I work with wounded partners, it is very common for them to attribute their partner's infidelity-related behavior to some sort of inadequacy on their part. But the truth of the matter is that infidelity always says more about the unfaithful partner than it does about the person they were unfaithful to. In my experience working with couples, I have found that

many people who cheat or look at pornography justify their behavior by citing some way(s) that their partner failed to meet their needs. However, what is typically at the root of the issue isn't their partner's shortcomings but their attitude of entitlement around what they think that their partner should be doing for them.

3. **The Fear of Change:** The fear of change is extremely common. For most people, I would describe this as more of a discomfort around change. However, depending on someone's background, it isn't uncommon for an actual fear of change to exist. As human beings, we are hardwired to resist change because of our aversion to loss. We tend to believe that the pain of loss, or even potential loss, resulting from the change(s) in our lives is going to be greater than whatever we could gain through embracing the change. Therefore, we resist change because we might lose something. In the case of infidelity, changes that we have no control over are thrust upon us, and the suddenness of this can make it difficult to accept and work through.

4. **Fear of Loneliness:** I see this one quite often in my coaching practice, especially when working with partners that should leave their mate but are hesitant to do so. This is understandable and very common. However, staying in a relationship with a partner that isn't willing or able to do their own recovery in order to deal with their infidelity-related behavior is not advisable. It will likely end up hurting you a lot more in the long run than being alone will. Fear of loneliness is closely linked to feelings of rejection, which are common after discovery or disclosure of infidelity.

5. **The Fear of Loss of Control:** Wounded partners almost always feel some sort of loss of control, which often results in fear. This is due to the fact that we have had the rug pulled out from under us in terms of what we have come to expect from our relationship and our partner's behavior. Discovery or disclosure of our partner's infidelity-related behavior leaves us feeling shattered. What we thought we knew and could count on turned out not to be the case. This can leave us with the feeling that nothing in our world makes sense anymore. This feeling creates a sense of losing control, which can create intense fear.

1. Could you relate to any of the common fears above? If so, which ones?

_____
_____
_____
_____
_____

2. If you answered "yes" to Question 1, are these fears affecting you? If so, how?

_____
_____
_____
_____
_____

Getting Stuck in Fear

Most of us have heard the phrase, "paralyzed with fear". Although the feeling of being paralyzed is a natural part of the fight or flight response, we can also stay paralyzed with fear long after a frightening event has passed. Trauma, such as the discovery of infidelity, can lead to intense feelings of anxiety. Excess anxiety can become a problem when it causes us to experience insomnia, headaches and other chronic pain, poor quality of life, social isolation, and difficulty functioning in our daily lives. Over time, we can become stuck here, which can cause us to avoid situations that we deem to be even remotely dangerous. This can result in an inability to grow in our recovery.

The most serious form of getting stuck in fear is anxiety disorder. Trauma, stress, and even our personalities can all make us susceptible to developing an anxiety disorder. Unfortunately, trauma and stress go hand in hand with the discovery of infidelity. You may want to consult with your doctor if you are displaying any of the following symptoms:

- Feeling restless or "wound up"
- Fatigue
- Irritability
- Difficulty concentrating
- Unexplained pain
- Sleep issues
- Chronic worry
- Pounding or racing heart
- Sweating
- Feelings of impending doom

Of course, these symptoms can appear after the discovery or disclosure of our partner's infidelity. However, it never hurts to consult with your physician, especially if any of the symptoms listed above feel unusually intense or have lasted for an extended period of time.

CHAPTER 18

Dealing With Fear

Living without fear is an impossibility, unless your amygdala has been damaged in a way that prevents you from feeling it. For most of us, fear is something that we have to live with. That being said, it doesn't have to limit us in what we need to or want to accomplish; but it takes some courage to overcome it. The word *courage* is defined as the "mental or moral strength to venture, persevere, or withstand danger, fear, or difficulty". (Merriam-Webster Dictionary).

The paradox in my coaching practice is that my clients often come to me with a heightened sense of fear because of what has transpired in their lives, and almost everything I ask them to do requires a significant amount of courage. This is particularly true if they are interested in overcoming the effects of infidelity in order to stay with their partner. For example, many wounded partners come to me saying that they want to stay with their partners yet are acting in ways that are tearing at the fabric of an already-fragile relationship. An example of this is using anger in the form of yelling, calling names, or shaming in order to mask vulnerable feelings such as fear, hurt, worry, and betrayal that lie just beneath the surface. While taking up a position of anger can provide a bit of cover for vulnerability, it's not honest if it is not the primary feeling we are experiencing. Therefore, this strategy will likely be unproductive. The solution to this is to share the feelings underneath the anger. This requires much courage because, in order to do it, one has to face their fear of being vulnerable after they have already been hurt so profoundly.

For some of us, fear can hold us back from making any decisions about the future of our relationship one way or the other. This can leave us feeling hopelessly torn. The reasons for staying or leaving vary from partner to partner, but here are some of the common issues that I see my clients facing:

1. Fear of losing family cohesiveness
2. Fear of financial ruin
3. Fear of the unknown
4. Fear of being alone
5. Fear of making personal changes needed to become independent
6. Fear of losing friends
7. Fear of judgment
8. Fear of displeasing God
9. Fear that forgiving their partner means excusing their partner's behavior

1. Do you feel stuck when it comes to deciding whether or not to stay in your current relationship? Why or why not?

_____
_____
_____
_____
_____

2. Could you relate to any of the common fears listed above? If so, which ones?

_____
_____
_____
_____
_____

3. If the fear(s) you face about staying or leaving your current relationship are different than the ones outlined above, list them here.

_____
_____
_____
_____

Even if you already know that you don't want to stay in your current relationship, it is still in your best interest to overcome your fears—especially those that were created because of what has happened. If you don't, fear can very easily become a limiting factor that will keep you from working toward what you want. Fear lends itself to making excuses that can cause us to give up before we even start, quit mid-way, or put us into a cycle of procrastination.

Whichever situation that you are currently in, let's look at some of the statements I hear from fearful clients on a regular basis that hold them back:

1. **This is going to be way too difficult:** I'm not going to lie; recovery from infidelity is definitely difficult. However, when a statement like this is made, it often enters our minds that it will be too difficult, so why even bother. Just because something is difficult, doesn't mean it's impossible. I see clients every day overcome the devastating effects of infidelity and achieve their goals, so I personally know that it is possible. In order to overcome difficulty, we must first acknowledge the difficulty and then figure out and strategize around what we need to do in order to overcome it. Depending on the goal, this could come in the form of learning how to communicate safely and productively, taking a class or joining a group, engaging with others who have made it through similar situations in order to learn from them, and/or hiring a counselor or coach to walk you through it.

2. **I'm afraid my efforts will fail:** While it's true that there are no guarantees in life, this type of statement almost ensures that we will never know if our efforts would have made a difference. That is because, by saying this, we are really excusing ourselves from trying. It's only natural that we

would be afraid to fail because so much is on the line. However, if we let this fear hold us back, we may be missing out on some serious personal growth. The answer to this situation is to set aside regular time for activities and work that support your personal recovery, the recovery of your relationship, or both, and work consistently and diligently toward your goals.

3. **This is going to take SO much work:** People who say this are not wrong. Mending from betrayal takes a tremendous amount of work. However, to quote Theodore Roosevelt, "Nothing worth having is ever achieved without effort." This is often a hard concept for wounded partners to accept because, since they didn't cause the damage to their relationship, they often resent the effort they have to put into mending it. This feeling of resentment is completely valid. However, we shouldn't let our resentments hold us back from what we want. Even if you are not resentful but simply feeling that it will be too much effort, remind yourself that any effort that you put toward your recovery will always be worth it because your wellbeing is important.

4. **If I have to schedule recovery, it feels like a chore:** I hear this one more often than you would think. Although it's somewhat related to #3, I felt it was different enough to include here. I'm always surprised at how many people don't see the value in scheduling activities related to recovery. The truth is that, when we engage in recovery, we are often learning many new skills at once. This takes time and practice. If we don't schedule it, our tendency will be to procrastinate or to avoid it. This is because recovery is uncomfortable and we, as human beings, don't like getting out of our comfort zone due to fear. Even if scheduling recovery does feel like a chore, I still encourage my clients to do it anyway. Scheduling recovery-related activities helps ensure that they get the priority they deserve.

5. **If I let my guard down, this will happen again:** I won't lie and tell you that this could never happen again. However, I can tell you that keeping your guard up could damage your current relationship or future relationships and it won't safeguard you from ever experiencing this again. Just as your partner's infidelity is 100% their responsibility, not yours, so is their recovery. I'm not advocating that you let your guard down in all areas

with someone who has proven to be untrustworthy and has yet to prove that they are serious about their recovery and amends. However, keeping your guard up and keeping an impenetrable wall up are two different things. Even though we are wounded, we have to let our guard down enough to be open to the possibility of change on our partner's part if we wish for the relationship to be reconciled.

6. **If I forgive my partner, they will get away with everything they have done:** This is a tough one because it is based on the human need for justice and/or revenge. It's a normal human response to situations in which others who were supposed to "play by the rules" chose not to do so. In our justice system, we have ways in which we can try to make right the wrongs others have done to us. In relationships, however, there is no such system. As a result, I frequently see wounded partners become judge, jury, and executioner when it comes to their unfaithful partners because if they don't, they know no one else will. The need for justice and/or revenge often drives them to "punish" their partner in order to feel some sort of relief from the outrage they feel. Here are some common ways that I have seen wounded partners try to right the wrong their partner has done to them by seeking revenge:

- Have a "revenge" affair
- Shame and/or ridicule their partner
- Bring up the infidelity-related behavior for years, or even decades
- Threaten their partner
- Deface or destroy property owned by their partner

The truth about revenge and/or seeking justice is that, while it can offer a small amount of temporary comfort, it will take a toll on us as wounded partners both physically and psychologically. Revenge, in particular, often births an endless cycle that can deplete our emotional energy and leave us feeling hollow. The appeal of revenge is that it offers us a satisfying "quick fix". Unfortunately, the satisfaction that we might feel is fleeting, leaving us with a need for further revenge. In the same way, seeking justice can leave us feeling depleted as well. As opposed to revenge, seeking justice in and of itself isn't particularly harmful. The issue is that, when it comes to infidelity, there really isn't a way to get justice because our partners can't offer us restitution for what they have done. If we spend our energy seeking justice where there is none, we risk depleting our emotional reserves in the process. The better focus for us as wounded partners is to require a reasonable amount of accountability from our partners moving forward.

A Word About "Revenge" Affairs

"Revenge proves its own executioner." —John Ford

In my coaching practice, I run across a fair number of people who entertain thoughts of having an affair or actually have an affair themselves after they discover that their partner has been unfaithful. Although this isn't particularly surprising, it is concerning to me since I witness the devastation infidelity causes to individuals and relationships on a daily basis.

Discovering that your partner has been unfaithful is one of the most immensely painful events that a person can go through. As I've established throughout this book, the trauma caused by infidelity creates a highly emotionally charged situation for the wounded partner. As a result, it's not surprising that many of us would entertain thoughts of getting back at our partner one way or another. If you think about it, a "revenge" affair can seem like the perfect way to do that… at least on the surface.

When I hear that someone has had an affair or is entertaining thoughts of one in response to their partner's infidelity-related behavior, it's typically for one of the following 3 reasons:

1. To hurt their partner as much as they were hurt or "even the score"

2. To teach their partner a lesson

3. To make their partner empathize with or understand the pain they are in

Although I certainly understand the reasoning, my experience working with betrayed partners and couples working through infidelity has shown me that the outcome is usually the exact opposite of what the wounded partner had in mind. This is for three main reasons:

1. The bond has already been severed. When your partner engaged in their affair or other infidelity-related behavior, one of the reasons it hurt you so badly is because there was an active bond between you and your partner, at least on your side of things. If you engage in a revenge affair, you will be unable to even the score because the impact of your actions won't have nearly the same effect on your partner as it did on you. Not to mention that many wounding partners lack the empathy to understand our feelings to begin with.

2. It can make the wounding partner feel justified in continuing their bad behavior. For some wounding partners, especially the unrepentant ones, the fact that their partner engaged in a revenge affair gives them just the excuse they need to carry on with their own bad behavior. For some, this means an excuse to continue their affair or other infidelity-related behavior. For others, it means giving them an excuse to minimize their actions, refuse to accept responsibility, or minimize the wounded partner's feelings.

What makes me sad about these situations is that, if reconciliation is the ultimate goal, revenge affairs complicate the process so much that it can take years to untangle all of the issues. The old adage "two wrongs don't make a right" definitely applies in this situation. In the case of infidelity, two wrongs make it worse.

If reconciliation is not your goal or is not possible, I still encourage you to think long and hard before retaliating with an affair of your own. Engagement in a revenge affair hurts the wounded partner's individual recovery in the following ways:

- The feeling of betrayal doesn't go away, but is compounded with guilt and shame

- Respect for ourselves weakens because we become like the person who hurt us

- It provides a distraction from emotions and trauma that need to be dealt with

- It causes many of us to go against our own morals and values

- If we have children, we set a poor example

Affairs and infidelity-related behavior leave a debt that simply can't be repaid. If your partner is willing to do the work, please take some time to decide if you think reconciliation is a possibility and don't engage in an affair of your own based on an emotionally charged situation. If, over time, your partner is still "not getting it" or hasn't chosen you, moving on in your life will be much easier without the guilt and shame that can result from retaliation.

1. What do you think of your partner's behavior? Have you lost respect for them? If you engage in a revenge affair, do you think you might feel the same way about yourself? Why or why not?

_____
_____
_____
_____
_____

2. Can you relate to any of the common excuses listed above? If so, which one(s)?

_____
_____
_____
_____
_____

3. If you answered "yes" to Question #2, in which ways do you think these excuses are holding you back?

_____
_____
_____
_____
_____

Facing and Overcoming Fear

Fear can be intense and overwhelming, but it doesn't have to hold you back if you don't want it to. That being said, it does take some practice and self-discipline to master. Here are some ways that you can practice facing and overcoming your fear:

1. Take a time-out: This tip is for when you are feeling the rush of adrenaline that often signals that fear is present. Decide ahead of time not to respond right away when you feel a surge of adrenaline hit your system. Instead, allow your sympathetic nervous system to calm down by distracting yourself and/or getting active. Walk around your neighborhood, take a bath, or listen to soothing music for at least 15 minutes before you respond.

2. Breathe: The activation of the sympathetic nervous system often causes an increase in breathing rate. Our breathing also tends to become shallow. We can counteract this, and calm ourselves down in the process, by taking deep, purposeful breaths. Next time you feel your breathing rate increase, practice breathing in deeply and slowly through the nose and out through the mouth until you feel calmer.

3. Name it: If you are to overcome your fear, it's first important to identify where that fear is coming from. After you have calmed down, take a moment to reflect on what is really going on inside of you. Journaling is particularly useful at this point because you can write down what comes to mind. Doing this will help you identify your fear(s).

4. Don't avoid it: Although avoidance of scary situations and feelings will likely offer you relief in the short term, studies have shown that avoidance of fearful situations, when practiced on a regular basis, can actually increase anxiety in the long term.

5. Sit with it: This is another time when journaling can be helpful. Write down your ideas around what the root cause of the fear could be. Is it fear of abandonment? Fear of failure? Fear of inadequacy?

6. Identify excuses: Are there any excuses you are making in order to keep yourself from dealing with the things you fear? If so, identify ways in which you can overcome them.

7. Write down the truth about your fear(s): Are you imagining worst-case scenarios? If so, this could be amplifying your fear(s). Take some time to write out the truth of the situation.

8. Decide what you're going to do: Now that you are calm, have identified what is bothering you, and have adjusted your perspective, it's time to act. Decide how you are going to respond to the situation — if a response is truly required. If you find that you are still not able to respond in a healthy way, take more time to reflect, calm down, and/or get your mind off of things.

9. Write down at least one fear that you have about your current situation.

_____
_____
_____
_____
_____

10. What do you think this fear is based on?

_____
_____
_____
_____
_____

11. Are there any excuses you are currently using to keep you from dealing with the situation in a healthy way? If so, what are they?

_____
_____
_____
_____
_____

12. Are you imagining worst-case scenarios with regard to your fear(s)? If so, write down what you are imagining.

_____
_____
_____
_____
_____

13. If you answered "yes" to Question #4, take some time to write down the truth about your situation.

_____
_____
_____
_____
_____

14. How do you think you could respond in a healthy way to address your fear(s)?

_____
_____
_____
_____
_____

CHAPTER 19

What is Forgiveness?

"Resentment is like drinking poison and then hoping it will kill your enemies." -Nelson Mandela

What is Forgiveness?

I want to start off by saying that this section isn't going to be as applicable to you as other chapters of this book if you are still in the discovery/disclosure phase of infidelity. This is not to say that the words and ideas contained in these chapters won't be worth reading. However, if you don't have a clear idea of what has transpired, it's best to hold off on trying to forgive until you have the full picture because you can't forgive what you aren't aware of. If you choose to read these chapters today, please be aware that it will likely be a lot more useful to you as a reference tool later in your journey. This section on forgiveness is most applicable to those of you who have been out of the discovery/disclosure phase for at least 6 months and are trying to find a way to move forward —with or without your partner.

The term "forgiveness" describes a person's conscious decision to let go of feelings of resentment and/or the need for revenge toward a person or people who have harmed them. Forgiveness is a personal decision that can happen whether or not the person or people being forgiven actually deserve it and/or are sorry for their behavior. Forgiveness is entirely different than reconciliation, which I will discuss in more detail later in this section.

When I talk to my clients about forgiveness, I like to use the analogy of debt. Let's say that a person who borrowed money from me owes me $500, but it becomes apparent for one reason or another that they will never be able to repay me. I could waste precious time and energy on trying to get them to repay me, but the fact of the matter is that the debt can't be repaid. I decided, for my own sake, to forgive the debt because I don't want to spend any more time on it. The person may or may not be sorry that they can't repay me, but that is irrelevant. I decided for my own sake to let it go because I determined that spending time and energy on something that couldn't be repaid was a poor use of my resources.

This scenario is similar to the debt owed to wounded partners when they learn of the wounding partner's infidelity. As sad as it is, infidelity creates a debt that can never be repaid. This is not to say that accountability isn't important, but that has more to do with reconciliation than it does with forgiveness. At some point, a wounded partner has to make a personal decision about whether they are going to try to make their partner "pay" for what they have done, or if they are going to give up the right to seek restitution and retribution for their partner's unfaithful actions. Based on my own personal experience as well as my experience with working with hundreds of wounded partners, I will tell you that trying to make someone pay for their misdeeds and/or be sorry for their actions is a waste of time and energy. The act of forgiveness is an internal matter. It isn't done for someone else, and it isn't done because someone is sorry (although hopefully they are). It is done for your own sake. The act of forgiveness allows you the opportunity to live with peace of mind and heart. It can give you the ability to put your partner's bad actions behind you and move forward, however you choose to do that, without the weight of those actions around your neck. It can also help you stay out of a powerless "victim" mentality, because forgiveness is a decision you use your internal power to make in order to move on from the actions of others. As such, it means that what someone did to you doesn't have to rule your life forever. *Forgiveness is the antidote to the corrosiveness of anger, resentment, and the need for vengeance.*

A Word About "Instant" Forgiveness

True forgiveness is difficult to achieve. As I will explain in the next section, it is a process and not a one-time event. True forgiveness isn't something that can be manufactured, and it's not something that can, or should, be decided upon quickly.

When I was young, we occasionally went camping. I remember watching my dad put out our campfire, and I noticed that he took several steps to accomplish that. First, he stopped adding the fuel that was keeping the fire going.

Next, he let the fire burn down so that the flames were much smaller. After that, he poured water on it. Then, he stirred the ashes of the fire to mix the water through.

Finally, he came back and checked the fire to make sure that it was out. If it was still going, he would repeat some of those steps.

The pain of our partner's infidelity creates a burning fire, and the process of forgiveness is like the steps my dad took to put the fire out. *Forgiveness is not water that you can pour over the raging fire of infidelity in hopes that it will snuff out the pain caused by it, nor the present and future damage done by it.* If the proper steps aren't taken to put out the fire, it is highly likely to resurface.

Although forgiveness is elusive and difficult for many of my clients, a handful of them seem to have the opposite issue. I have had a number of clients in my office that tell me that they have already forgiven their partner's infidelity-related behavior within months, weeks, days, and even a few hours of discovering their infidelity. This is not to say that you can't have a willingness to consider forgiveness now. However, I must warn you that forgiving too quickly will only set you up for heartache and frustration later on. I wish I had better news to tell you but, the truth is, there is simply no shortcut to forgiveness.

My experience has led me to conclude that my clients offer forgiveness too soon for the following reasons:

- They receive messages from friends, family, religious leaders, or coaches or counselors that they must forgive right away.
- They feel pressured by the wounding partner's need to be forgiven and/or the wounding partner is actively pressuring them to forgive.

- They are putting pressure on themselves to forgive.

- They are forgiving in an attempt to escape their pain.

Let's take a look at each one of these more closely:

1. **They receive messages from friends, family, coaches or counselors, or religious leaders that they must forgive right away.** Unfortunately, this is quite common. Well-meaning family, friends, religious leaders, and even coaches and counselors can send the message that if you would only forgive, everything would get better. This isn't accurate and, although they mean well, I would advise you to disregard their advice in this matter. Additionally, if someone tells you that nothing will get better until you forgive or that your pain is an indication of unforgiveness, I urge you to disregard this type of advice as well. Although most people who give this type of advice are well-meaning, there are also some who will shame you for not forgiving soon after the infidelity. What I would say to that is there's a difference between having an attitude of forgiveness and actually forgiving. An attitude of being open to forgiveness is something to strive for. Instantaneous forgiveness is unrealistic and damaging to everyone involved.

2. **They feel pressured by the wounding partner's need to be forgiven and/or the wounding partner is actively pressuring them to forgive.** Although it's certainly understandable that your partner may want to be forgiven, I advise you to hold off on saying that you forgive them until you are truly ready. The guilt felt by your partner for what they have done to you and the relationship is theirs to deal with, not yours. If your partner is pressuring you to "get over it" or "just forgive," this is actually a red flag. I have seen many wounding partners do this in an attempt to alleviate their own suffering. While I never advocate for wounded partners to hold forgiveness over the wounding partner's head as a way to make them pay, it's not appropriate for you to forgive them at the expense of your own wellbeing — which is what you would be doing. If you are dealing with either of these two scenarios, my advice would be to answer with, "I want to forgive you, and I'm working toward it. However, I'm not there yet." If your partner persists, you may need to enlist expert help in order to help them to understand why this isn't appropriate.

3. They are putting pressure on themselves to forgive. In my experience, some wounded partners put a large amount of pressure on themselves to forgive. This is typically because either, a) they want to adhere to the requirements of their religion, or b) they want to ensure that the relationship makes it. Although there may be other reasons as well, these are the two most common reasons that I see in my office. While I appreciate the desire to adhere to religious requirements, Bible verses dealing with forgiveness are often misinterpreted. Although it's true that God forgives us instantaneously, I would ask you to remember that God has abilities that you and I do not. While we can ask God to help us to eventually forgive, we can also rest assured that God understands our human struggles and limitations.

When partners want to forgive so that the relationship makes it, it is usually because a) they fear how their anger and hurt might damage their relationship, or b) their partner is unrepentant and has threatened to withdraw or leave if they don't let it go. Although it's understandable that some of us fear how our pain might influence us to react, I can assure you that instantaneous forgiveness does nothing to fix our feelings. If your partner is unrepentant or threatening physical and/or emotional abandonment, this is inappropriate and abusive. Unfortunately, this is not uncommon in relationships, especially if the wounding partner is an addict, intimacy avoidant, or intimacy anorexic®. If this describes your situation, please reach out to a coach or counselor who is trained in this area to help you remain strong in your boundaries. Help can also be found at www.coda.org for those of you who may be struggling with codependency.

4. They are forgiving in an attempt to escape their pain. Unfortunately, forgiveness is not a magic pill we can take to escape the pain our partner's actions have caused us. Just like in the analogy of the fire I used above; the fire caused by the pain of infidelity needs to be carefully tended in order to ensure that it doesn't reignite later on. If you remain in denial about the ways in which your partner's actions have affected you, you will only delay and/or prolong your pain.

In my experience, wounded partners who forgive too quickly set themselves up for pitfalls later on. Here are some of the ways that forgiving too soon can affect us:

1. We stuff our emotions. Stuffing emotions, especially the intense emotions resulting from infidelity, can cause a myriad of problems to our mental, spiritual, and physical health. Studies have linked repressed emotions to depression, anxiety, heart disease, digestive issues, and more.

2. We set ourselves up for unnecessary guilt later on. Instantaneous forgiveness is not real forgiveness. When we say we forgive our partner and then realize we still have pain and anger, we can be setting ourselves up for self-criticism and/or judgement. I have had numerous partners come to me because they felt guilty about not forgiving their partner's infidelity-related behavior. The issue with instant forgiveness is that we can only forgive what we are aware of at a particular moment in time. This isn't possible in the case of infidelity because wounded partners experience new awareness of its effects for months and years beyond discovery/disclosure. This is a normal part of the recovery process.

3. We send confusing messages to our partner. When we tell our partner that we forgive them and then struggle with our feelings later on, we send confusing messages. It would be better to tell them that we will try to work toward forgiveness than that we have totally forgiven them. As I stated previously, it's a normal part of a wounded partner's recovery process to become newly aware of pain resulting from their partner's actions months and years after discovery/disclosure of the infidelity. Forgiveness will be an ongoing process as new realizations come to light and bring new pain with them.

4. We deny ourselves the ability to explore our pain. We can feel the pain of betrayal for numerous reasons. Wounded partners can feel pain from the actual betrayal, the fact that our partner shared intimacy with someone other than us, being gaslit, being lied to, and more. Forgiving your partner too quickly will be detrimental to your healing in the long run. It takes time to dissect our partner's betrayal in order to identify and deal with each of the areas that the pain is coming from.

5. We let the wounding partner off the hook too easily. Let me preface this by stating that I am not advocating for you to hold forgiveness over your partner's head in order to make them pay. However, letting your partner off the hook by telling them you forgive them too soon can backfire. Your partner needs to do their own recovery work and forgiving them too soon can send the message that they don't need to take what they did seriously.

Although I advocate for partners to forgive when they are ready, forgiveness is an item of high value and should never be handed out cheaply. Our willingness to forgive our partner's egregious behavior is an act of mercy. It is at the core of who we are as people. Once we forgive, we are relinquishing our right to future retribution and/or restitution. This is important, and it costs us something. Although the idea that that we can make our partners pay by refusing to forgive them is an erroneous one, it doesn't mean that our willingness to extend forgiveness to them is worthless or should be offered lightly.

1. Do you feel that you may have forgiven your partner too quickly? Why or why not?

_____
_____
_____
_____

2. If you answered "yes" to Question #1, list some of the ways this is currently costing you and/or ways it might cost you in the future.

_____
_____
_____
_____

CHAPTER 20

What Forgiveness Isn't and Practical Steps to Forgiveness

As important as it is to talk about what forgiveness is, it is equally as important to talk about what it isn't. When I get pushback from clients on the concept of forgiveness, it is almost always because they have misconceptions about what it means to forgive. Here is a list of some of the things forgiveness is not:

- A one-time event
- The same as forgetting about what happened
- An obligation to reconcile
- The same as extending trust
- Agreeing with, excusing, condoning, or denying your partner's bad behavior
- A feeling
- The same as tolerating bad behavior
- Only a religious practice

Let's look at each one of these in greater detail:

1. Forgiveness is not a one-time event. Forgiveness is more of a process than a one-time event. You can decide to forgive someone but still have times when you remember the pain and are angry about it. Just because you feel hurt, sad, and angry about what has happened doesn't mean that you don't forgive your partner. If you are working toward forgiveness, reestablish your commitment to forgive each time you have painful memories so that bitterness, anger, and resentment don't take over.

2. Forgiveness is not the same as forgetting about what happened. Just as the ability to sense danger has helped the human race survive, so has the ability to remember traumatic events. Our brains are wired to remember painful and/or dangerous situations so that we can learn from them. You will always remember what has happened. However, the purpose of forgiveness is to allow you to remember without being taken over by the emotions that accompany your memories.

3. Forgiveness is not an obligation to reconcile. Although forgiveness is a key component of reconciliation, to forgive someone doesn't necessarily mean that you are ready, willing, or able to reconcile with that person. Remember that forgiveness is for you more than it is for the other person. When we forgive, we are freeing ourselves from the pain that resentment and bitterness can cause for us in the future. It does not mean that we need to stay with a person who was unfaithful to us if we don't want to or aren't able to.

4. Forgiveness is not the same as extending trust. As I established earlier, forgiveness can be extended even when someone refuses to apologize or change their behavior. This does not hold true when extending trust. In order to trust someone again after they have proven to be unfaithful, we need to see tangible evidence of change on their part. We need to know that they are sorry for what they have done and understand how their actions have affected us. We also need to evaluate their actions over time in order to determine whether or not they are committed to doing whatever it takes to keep themselves from betraying us again. Confusing forgiveness and trust can put you in a high-risk situation where you are likely to be hurt again.

5. Forgiveness is not agreeing with, excusing, condoning, or denying your partner's bad behavior. In my experience, this is the number one reason that wounded partners have trouble with the concept of forgiveness. When we forgive, we are releasing the right to restitution and/or revenge for our own mental health. However, for many of us, it is important to understand who or what we are releasing those rights to. For some of us, we are releasing our rights to God. For others, our rights to vengeance and restitution go to our Higher Power or the Universe. Whomever or whatever you release your rights to, it's important for many of us to believe that it will be made right somehow in the end. For those of us with no Higher Power, understanding that someone's bad actions do not make up the totality of their being is a way we can begin the path to forgiveness. It can also be helpful to understand that, when someone acts without integrity, their attitudes and actions usually end up costing them in one way or another down the line.

6. Forgiveness is not a feeling. As I stated earlier, forgiveness is a conscious choice to let go of feelings of resentment and/or the need for revenge. If we wait until we "feel" forgiving, that feeling may never come. Forgiveness is a personal choice, and, as such, must be made by each individual when the time is right. If you are suffering from the effects of your anger and resentment, it is probably time to contemplate forgiveness for your own sake. Additionally, since it is a choice, you can choose more than once to forgive as bitter and painful memories come up for you over time. As I stated previously, forgiveness is a process, not a one-time event.

7. Forgiveness is not the same as tolerating bad behavior. Deciding to forgive someone only means that you are relinquishing your rights to restitution and vengeance for their past actions, not excusing their ongoing bad behavior. It's important that we observe our partner's behavior in order to determine if we should stay with them or not. Excusing and tolerating continued infidelity-related behavior and/or abuse is never advisable. **Forgiveness is not a license for our partner to treat us with ongoing callousness and disrespect.**

8. Forgiveness is not only a religious practice. Although the concept of forgiveness can be found in a wide variety of religious belief systems, it is not only for religious people. There are many people who have no specific religious affiliation who see forgiveness as a virtue that is helpful to the person doing the forgiving. From a mental-health standpoint, most psychologists agree that dropping anger and resentment is healthier for an individual than letting it eat away at them over time.

1. Are you open to considering forgiveness of your partner's actions as an option for you now or in the future? Why or why not?

_____
_____
_____
_____
_____

1. Out of the things listed above regarding what forgiveness is not, which one stands out to you the most? Why is it important?

_____
_____
_____
_____
_____

The Benefits of Forgiveness

Forgiveness can benefit a person in every area of their life. Here are some key benefits that you could reap as you work toward forgiveness:

1. **Physical Benefits:** Multiple studies, including those from Johns Hopkins and The Mayo Clinic, have revealed that hanging onto hurt,

disappointment, and resentment can affect our health in negative ways. Chronic anger, for example, puts the body into fight or flight mode which, as I have established in earlier sections, causes changes within our body that affect heart rate and blood pressure. Prolonged exposure to the hormones and adrenaline released in the fight or flight response can affect how our immune system recognizes and fights bacteria, viruses, toxins, and other potentially harmful substances. Forgiveness can provide physical benefits such as lower blood pressure, reduced risk for heart disease, better sleep, and reduced levels of pain. It can also result in a stronger immune system and fewer symptoms of depression.

2. **Emotional/Mental Benefits:** I think most of us understand that releasing resentments can help us emotionally and mentally. Studies have shown that forgiveness can benefit us with reduced levels of depression and anxiety and reduced stress. Without high levels of anxiety and anger, we can turn our emotional energy to more productive things like self-care and self-compassion. It is hard, if not impossible, to heal ourselves when we hold onto bitterness and resentment. We may not realize it, but unforgiveness can become a heavy weight that we get used to carrying around. It isn't until we set it down that we realize how heavy it has become.

3. **Relationship Benefits:** If we are to move forward in recovery with a partner who has been unfaithful, it is clear that forgiveness is the beginning of a path to reconciliation. If you are staying with your partner, a lack of forgiveness on your part will likely result in increased levels of disharmony and distance with your partner throughout the life of the relationship. If you don't plan on staying in your current relationship, an attitude of forgiveness toward the one who betrayed you can provide you with benefits in your next relationship. Bringing anger and resentment into a new relationship can result in a broken connection between you and your new partner, and a focus on the past can prevent you from enjoying your new relationship. Additionally, developing an ability to forgive can benefit you and your loved ones because you will be less likely to hold grudges.

4. **Spiritual Benefits:** Holding onto anger and resentment can cause us to feel at odds with ourselves, our beliefs, and God. Whether you have

chosen a specific religion or not, forgiveness can lead to a lightness of spirit, and a spiritual experience of peace and love. It can also lead to increased understanding, compassion, and empathy.

1. Out of the ways that forgiveness can benefit us listed above, which one(s) is/are the most appealing to you? Why do you think that is?

_____
_____
_____
_____
_____

Practical Steps to Forgiveness

Forgiveness isn't easy. In fact, it may be one of the hardest things you will ever choose to do. Even so, I hope you can see that there are many benefits to be gained through forgiving your partner even if you don't choose to reconcile with them. Here are some practical steps that you can take as you move toward forgiveness:

1. **Recognize ways in which your anger and resentment are costing you.** Although anger is a normal part of the grieving process, there is always a point where we realize that our anger is doing more harm than good. Ask yourself what you are truly gaining by holding onto anger and resentments. If the answer is "nothing" or "not much", you may want to consider forgiveness as an alternative. If you are telling yourself that holding onto your anger and resentment will ensure that your partner pays for what they have done, consider this quote by Lawrence Douglas Wilder — "Anger doesn't solve anything. It builds nothing, but it can destroy everything."

2. **Identify who and what needs to be forgiven.** We can't forgive what we don't acknowledge and/or aren't aware of. Grieving our losses is an essential prerequisite to forgiveness because we need to truly understand what has happened to us as a result of our partner's infidelity before we can hope to forgive it.

3. **Consider the benefits of forgiving.** The personal and relational benefits of forgiveness are numerous. Try to focus on how forgiving your partner can be beneficial to you and/or your relationship.

4. **Make a choice to forgive.** Remember, forgiveness is a choice, not a feeling. Make forgiveness a goal and actively work toward it every day. When anger and resentments arise, it is okay to acknowledge them. However, it is important to remind yourself that you have decided to forgive your partner so that the anger and resentments don't take root and grow.

5. **Choose to focus on what is helpful.** As we move along in the forgiveness process, our focus on the pain of the past can offer diminishing returns. When your mind starts ruminating on your partner's infidelity-related behavior, ask yourself if it is helping you or hurting you. Spending too much time rehashing the past can sabotage you on your journey to forgiveness.

6. **Try to develop empathy and compassion for your partner.** Empathy and compassion are important ingredients of forgiveness. Putting yourself in your partner's shoes to at least try to understand how their faulty thinking or traumatic background contributed to their choices can be tough, but it will help you forgive them more easily. I don't say this to try and get you to feel sorry for them or excuse their behavior in any way. However, someone suffering from faulty thinking due to addiction or trauma isn't likely to make the best choices. It may help you on your path to forgiveness to realize that.

7. **Enlist some help.** As I stated above, forgiveness is really tough and, sometimes, we need a bit of extra help getting there. Journaling, prayer, and guided meditation around forgiveness can help us have more success. Additionally, talking to a coach, counselor, spiritual leader, family member, or trusted friend who has our best interests at heart can help us reach our goals of forgiveness.

8. **Have patience with yourself.** Understanding that forgiveness is a process will help you to be patient with yourself. The pain from infidelity is so profound that it may take months or even years for you to reach a place of forgiveness. It is normal for residual pain, anger, and resentment

to crop up throughout the process. Don't use these "flare-ups" as an excuse to get stuck— but do be patient with yourself when you have to revisit certain memories and recommit to the process of forgiveness.

I would like to add here that, in my coaching practice, I have seen partners who are suddenly struggling with forgiveness several years after reconciling with their partner. This is confusing to them because they thought they had forgiven their partner and are now worried that they have failed to forgive. If this describes you, I will tell you that it is normal to struggle with forgiveness at a certain point after reconciliation has taken place. In my experience, this struggle tends to happen at the 3-5-year mark but can take place anywhere along the journey. A sudden struggle with forgiveness doesn't mean you never forgave your partner. It has more to do with the fact that we can only forgive things that we are aware of. It's normal to become aware of new things along the way and have to forgive and even grieve them. Although this can be unpleasant for many of us, please understand that it's completely normal. You can get through this new phase using the same tools for forgiveness described above. Remember that recovery is a journey, not a destination, and have patience with yourself.

9. **Take care of yourself.** You may wonder what self-care has to do with forgiveness. Quite a lot, actually. If we are constantly worn out and depleted, this can add to our anger. This anger can put us in a mood where we are less likely to stay committed to our decision to forgive. Instead, we may feel like punishing our partner for putting us in this position. The practice of self-care is a way that we can give back to ourselves during trying times.

10. **Forgive yourself.** None of us is perfect. As I said before, forgiveness is a process. If you have bad days when you don't feel like forgiving, try to get back on track as soon as possible and forgive yourself for not doing it perfectly.

11. **Beware of a self-righteous attitude.** Earlier in the book, I referred to the concept of grandiosity. According to psychologist Terry Real, grandiosity is defined as "contempt for others". In his book Fierce Intimacy, he describes the attitude of a grandiose person as the drive to frequently "one-up" others. In the case of wounded partners, grandiosity

can be an issue because we truly do have the moral high ground when it comes to fidelity. However, a "one-up" attitude will sabotage us in our efforts to forgive.

1. Do you think your anger and resentment could be costing you emotionally, physically, relationally, or spiritually? If so, list the ways in which it may be harming you.

_____
_____
_____
_____
_____

2. List some of the benefits you could get from choosing to forgive your partner. If you are staying in your relationship, list the relational benefits as well.

_____
_____
_____
_____
_____

3. Make a list of the people in your life whom you might consider forgiving, including your partner, on the left-hand side of the table below. On the right-hand side, list what you need to forgive each person for.

4. Read the list you made in Question #3. Do you think you could make a choice to forgive each person? If not, why not? If so, why do you think forgiveness would be beneficial?

_____
_____
_____
_____

5. Do you think you might be spending too much time rehashing past events? Why or why not?

_____
_____
_____
_____

6. What are some of the factors that you can see in your partner's background that might have contributed to their poor decisions?

_____
_____
_____
_____

7. If you have decided to forgive, make a list of people whom you can trust to support you as you try to forgive.

_____
_____
_____
_____

8. If you have not made a choice to forgive yet, but are considering it, make a list of people that would give you sound advice about your hesitancy to forgive.

_____
_____
_____
_____
_____

9. Are you feeling depleted? Why or why not? Can you identify ways in which you could better care for yourself?

_____
_____
_____
_____
_____

10. Do you have things in your life that you haven't forgiven yourself for? What are they? Do you think you could forgive yourself? Why or why not?

_____
_____
_____
_____
_____

11. Do you think that grandiosity is a problem for you? Why or why not? If so, make a list of ways that you are trying to "one-up" when interacting with your partner and/or others.

_____
_____
_____
_____
_____

CHAPTER 21

Reconciliation

I believe there has been quite an error made, especially in religious circles, when it comes to forgiveness and reconciliation. The message often given to wounded partners is that they are being unforgiving if they don't choose to or don't know if they want to reconcile with an unfaithful partner. This is simply not true. As I explained above, you can forgive someone regardless of whether they are sorry for their actions because forgiveness is a personal choice based on the need or desire to let anger and resentment go. This is not true of reconciliation, which is completely dependent on actions. *The main difference between forgiveness and reconciliation is that forgiveness is something we choose to do regardless of the other person's attitudes and actions, while true reconciliation requires forgiveness plus action. Forgiveness is a component of reconciliation but does not guarantee it if both people aren't willing to do what it takes in order to reconcile the relationship.* If a wounded partner chooses not to reconcile with the wounding partner, they likely have very good reasons for their choice. To say that a wounded partner who is unable to reconcile with an unfaithful partner is being unforgiving is incorrect at best and, at worst, unfair and cruel.

If you look up the word "reconcile" in the dictionary, you will see that it means "to restore to friendship or harmony". (Merriam-Webster). In order to do this, multiple things have to take place over an extended period of time. I would like to add here that merely "staying together" after infidelity does not qualify as reconciliation if the relationship is riddled with shaming, defensiveness, fighting, and distrust. The key to reconciliation is truly in its definition — a restoration of friendship and harmony.

As I wrote in the paragraph above, in order for reconciliation to truly take place, multiple things must happen over an extended period of time. In my experience, couples break up more often over how discussions around the infidelity are handled than around the infidelity itself. Here is a list of things that, in my experience, are necessary if a relationship is to truly be reconciled:

- The infidelity-related behavior must stop
- The wounding partner must be willing to divulge all of the facts surrounding any infidelity-related behavior
- The wounding partner must show remorse for what they have done
- The wounding partner must not defend and must listen with empathy
- The wounded partner must be open to forgiveness
- The wounding partner must be accountable for their past and future actions
- The wounded partner must get their anger under control
- Both parties must have patience with the process
- Both parties must be consistent
- The wounded partner must actively engage in their own recovery
- Both parties must learn how to effectively deal with triggers and reminders
- Both parties must agree to be vulnerable
- Both parties must learn how to talk about the infidelity in an open and productive manner
- Both parties should seek outside, infidelity-specific help

Let's take a closer look at each one of these points:

1. The infidelity-related behavior must stop. This seems like a no-brainer, but you would be surprised at how many couples come to me expecting to make progress when the unfaithful partner is unwilling or unable to decide whether or not they want to end an affair, quit looking at pornography, etc. In my experience, it is impossible for a relationship to truly be reconciled when the wounding partner refuses to stop acting in ways that hurt their partner.

2. The wounding partner must be willing to divulge all of the facts surrounding any infidelity-related behavior. Besides ending the infidelity-related behavior, a willingness on the wounded partner's part to "come clean" about their unfaithful actions is one of the biggest determining factors as to whether or not a relationship can be reconciled. Earlier in this book, I described how damaging "dribbling" disclosure and/or withholding information from a wounded partner can be because, each time new information is received, it creates a new trauma for the one receiving it. Over time, this can become so damaging that the wounded partner's ability to reconcile or even to recover can be greatly diminished.

3. The wounding partner must show remorse for what they have done. When it comes to reconciliation, this point is just as important as divulging all of the information regarding the infidelity-related behavior. If a wounding partner can't show remorse for what they have done on a regular basis, hopes for reconciliation will be greatly reduced.

4. The wounding partner must not defend and must listen with empathy. The wounding partner's ability to listen with empathy and not defend themselves is another important factor when it comes to reconciliation. The process of recovery after infidelity is long and difficult. Defensiveness and a lack of empathy on the wounding partner's part will only cause the wounded partner to have doubts about whether or not their partner is truly remorseful.

5. The wounded partner must be open to forgiveness. This is a tough one for many wounded partners to accept. However, if your relationship is to truly be restored to friendship and harmony, an attitude of unforgiveness will surely stand in the way of that. While forgiveness doesn't guarantee reconciliation, it is necessary if reconciliation is going to have a chance. As I said earlier, forgiveness doesn't mean excusing, condoning, or forgetting what has transpired. However, without forgiveness, we are likely to prevent ourselves and our relationship from moving forward by harboring anger and resentment.

6. The wounding partner must be accountable for their past, present, and future actions. A lack of willingness on the wounding partner's part to be accountable for what they have done by admitting their actions, showing remorse, and attempting to understand how their actions have affected their partner will make it difficult for the relationship to be truly reconciled. Furthermore, a willingness to be held accountable for future actions is a must in order to reestablish trust.

7. The wounded partner must get their anger under control. As we discussed in Section 5, unbridled anger in the form of yelling, cursing, shaming, threatening, etc. will be just as damaging to a relationship after infidelity has occurred as it would have been prior to it. Although anger and even rage are completely understandable reactions to our circumstances, we must commit to making a serious effort to communicate our intense emotions in appropriate ways.

8. Both parties must have patience with the process. Recovery from the effects of infidelity is a long and trying process. On average, a couple recovering from an affair takes about 2 years to get to a point where reconciliation seems possible, and recovery is well underway. The process is full of ups and downs. A lot of it is repetitive, especially question-asking from the wounded partner about the infidelity. This can seem defeating at times. Patience with ourselves as well as with our partner is required as we travel the road to recovery.

9. Both parties must be consistent. When I talk to couples about rebuilding trust after infidelity, I explain how consistency plays a vital role in reconciliation. This includes consistent efforts around communication, accountability, and any other recovery behavior that has been agreed upon such as attending meetings, working specific programs, etc.

10. The wounded partner must actively engage in their own recovery. As wounded partners, we sustain traumatic injuries from the discovery of our partner's infidelity-related behavior. As nice as it would be to let our partners fix what they broke, it simply doesn't work that way. When clients ask me why they have to do recovery even though they did nothing to cause the situation, I like to use the analogy of getting hit while crossing the road. If a car hits us, even if we are in the crosswalk and minding our own business, we will sustain injuries that may require surgery, physical therapy, etc. If we don't do what it takes to address those injuries, we may never regain full use of our bodies. In the same way, injuries sustained from traumatic events can affect us in every area of our lives. If these aren't properly addressed, we will likely have problems functioning personally, relationally, emotionally, and spiritually.

11. Both parties must learn how to effectively deal with triggers and reminders. Unfortunately, triggers and reminders are a normal part of the process when it comes to infidelity recovery. It is not uncommon for wounded partners to experience 100 or more triggers per day in the weeks and months following discovery or disclosure of infidelity. If the wounding partner defends, blames, or acts unempathetically or annoyed, the wounded partner will be further injured, making reconciliation less likely. If the wounded partner doesn't learn to voice their anger, disappointment, hurt, and fear without inflicting damage, it will be hard for the relationship to recover.

12. Both parties must agree to be vulnerable. Let me qualify this statement by saying that I am not referring to a situation in which you as the wounded partner open yourself back up to a partner who hasn't proven themselves trustworthy. What I am saying is that we as wounded partners need to be honest and open about our true feelings without using anger as a smokescreen for more vulnerable emotions. Vulnerability on the wounding partner's part means no blaming, defending, or stonewalling when it comes to communication. Also, they must let down their pride and become willing to be accountable to their partner and to others.

13. Both parties must learn to talk about the infidelity in an open and productive manner. Most therapists and coaches agree that couples should openly talk about affairs and/or any other infidelity-related behavior. Research has even shown that couples who can talk about such things have higher success rates when it comes to staying together. That being said, it is imperative that communication around these matters be productive. If the conversations are fraught with defending, yelling, calling names, denial, stonewalling, and/or a lack of transparency, talking about it will likely do more harm than good.

14. Both parties should seek outside, infidelity-related help. While family counseling is good for many different situations, couples and individuals who are facing the aftermath of infidelity are dealing with specific issues that many counselors and coaches aren't adequately trained to deal with. Talking to a coach or counselor that has experience and training specifically around infidelity, sex addiction, and other related issues will be much more helpful to you on your path to reconciliation.

1. In your own words, describe the difference between forgiveness and reconciliation.

_____
_____
_____
_____
_____

2. Out of the 14 things that make reconciliation possible that are your responsibility, which ones are you willing to do? Which ones are you having a hard time with?

_____
_____
_____
_____
_____

3. Out of the 14 items/actions listed above that make reconciliation possible that are your partner's responsibility, which ones are they currently doing? Which ones are they currently not doing?

_____
_____
_____
_____

How Do I Know if I Should Pursue Reconciliation?

When I work with clients, this question is one of the most common questions I am asked. I wish I had a better answer, but the truth is that I can't tell anyone exactly when they should stay and when it's time to leave. I can, however, give some advice based on my experience working with couples and individuals suffering from the negative impacts of infidelity. I would suggest that you consider the following pieces of advice when you are trying to understand whether or not reconciliation is truly possible:

1. Give yourself time to decide. Finding out that your partner has been unfaithful creates intense pain. While it's normal to want to escape that pain, leaving the relationship soon after you discover your partner's infidelity may not be the best choice for you in the long run. When our minds are clouded with pain, anger, outrage, and humiliation it's impossible to make a rational decision. If a temporary separation is what you need to get your mind around what has happened, by all means do that. However, my best advice to you is to give yourself enough time to calm down in order to decide what it is you truly want.

2. Consider the attitudes and actions of your partner. The best relationship outcomes I have witnessed always start with the wounding partner displaying grief over what they have done. Anything less than a willingness to end the infidelity-related behavior and become accountable, honest, and transparent moving forward doesn't bode well for reconciliation. If your partner isn't willing to end the affair or other infidelity-related behavior, listen to you with empathy, and become accountable to you and to others, my advice would be to give them a short window of time (6-12 months) to come to their senses. If they don't change their ways within that time frame, it may be best for you to consider moving on.

Here are some common warning signs that I see from wounding partners that ultimately make healing virtually impossible for the wounded partner:

- An unwillingness to apologize for the betrayal
- An unwillingness to participate in coaching or counseling
- An unwillingness to do recovery work
- Continued lying
- Refusal to take responsibility for their actions
- Blaming the partner or others for their behavior

3. Consider the history of your relationship. This can be a challenge due to the fact that wounded partners tend to see the relationship in a negative light once infidelity is discovered. Once you have reached a calm state, I encourage you to make a pros and cons list for your relationship. Create a document and list all of the positive things about your relationship on one side and all of the negative things on the other. If you find that your relationship has quite a few positives, you may consider sticking around to see if reconciliation is possible. In my experience, the more positives a relationship had prior to the infidelity or still has, the more likely reconciliation will be.

4. Understand your own baggage. Let me preface this part by stating that infidelity is never the fault of the wounded partner. Your partner's choice to be unfaithful is 100% their responsibility. That being said, it is helpful for reconciliation when we understand what our emotional baggage is and when we might be reacting out of it. For example, if you are someone who tends to personalize things, it is possible that you are personalizing your partner's behavior. In my experience, wounded partners who attribute their partner's actions to perceived shortcomings or flaws on their part feel a higher level of pain than those who don't. Another example would be that if you are a person who has power and control issues, your anger could be amplified by the fact that you perceive your partner's choices to have taken power away from you. In my experience, a need for power often creates grandiose behavior in which the wounded partner will try to punish or control their partner in order to regain control.

CHAPTER 22

Letting Go of the Past

As with other parts of this book, this portion is only for those of you who have moved through the disclosure/discovery phase and feel ready to tackle the tough subject of forgiveness. The idea of letting go of the past is premature if you are only weeks or months out from discovering your partner's infidelity. Generally speaking, letting go of the past is appropriate at around 18 months to 2 years, and in some cases later, if you are staying together with your partner. If you aren't, it could probably be done sooner. As with other parts of this book, you can choose to skip this chapter altogether and refer back to it at a later time.

While letting go of the past requires forgiveness, I felt that it was different enough to warrant its own section. I believe that forgiveness is the beginning of letting go of the past, but not the end of it. Letting go requires a level of personal healing that can only be achieved with much time and consistent effort.

In my experience, there are several reasons why partners have trouble letting go of the past:

- Not enough time has gone by
- A failure to properly grieve losses caused by the infidelity
- A need to do more personal recovery

- The wounding partner has not helped them heal
- New information is discovered
- Overt triggers and reminders
- Attempting to control the wounding partner
- Rumination
- PTSD

Let's take a look at each one of these in further detail:

1. Not enough time has gone by. As I said at the beginning of this section, the idea of letting go of the past is premature for those of us who are still in the middle of disclosure/discovery. Infidelity is one of the most painful experiences a person can go through. As such, it takes time to process and heal from having our heart broken. If you are still in the process of learning the nature of your partner's infidelity or are days, weeks, or months out, please hold off on trying to forgive and let go. Concentrating on your own recovery is more appropriate for the early stages of infidelity recovery. Also, please understand that it can take months and years of consistent effort to let go of the past after having experienced the pain of infidelity.

2. A failure to properly grieve losses caused by the infidelity. For many of us, a failure to grieve can center around an inability to accept our new reality. Prior to the infidelity, you had a picture of what your relationship was, and your partner's unfaithful actions don't fit into that picture. It can be difficult to acknowledge and accept that the infidelity has now become part of the story of your relationship. For others, it can be because we simply haven't taken the time to count our losses and understand what those losses mean to us.

3. A need to do more personal recovery. It's not uncommon for wounded partners to come to me and feel that their unfaithful partner needs to do 100% of the work. I have covered this in other sections, but I would like to reiterate that it is extremely important for you to do your own recovery work as a wounded partner. Traumatic emotional injury is very serious and will cause you problems if not addressed properly. Another common reason why this becomes an issue is that we can get stuck on the tougher issues of recovery. Anger and resentment is the hardest area for most wounded partners to work on and usually needs to be revisited multiple times before it is resolved. Additionally, wounded partners who attribute their partner's behavior to their own shortcomings and perceived flaws (personalization) tend to have to revisit this area several times before they can move on.

4. The wounding partner has not helped them heal. I come across a fair percentage of wounded partners who beat themselves up for not being able to move on when, in reality, the wounding partner is not making it easy for them to do so. Any number of behaviors on the wounding partner's part can not only make it hard for us to feel safe but can also be re-traumatizing. An unwillingness to be accountable, apologize, or acknowledge our feelings are all re-wounding behaviors. Additionally, if our partner defends themselves or refuses to listen to our feelings with empathy, it will make it difficult for us to heal.

5. New information is discovered. If we find out new information about our partner's infidelity, we are highly likely to become re-traumatized. If our partner will not get honest with us and keeps "dribbling" out information, we may need to consider if it would be best for us to leave the situation. Also, I advise that once you have sufficient information about what your partner did, that you stop asking questions about the details surrounding your partner's infidelity. Prolonged discovery can re-traumatize you and make it difficult to let go and move on to a new phase. This is very difficult for many wounded partners to do, but it is the most helpful advice I can give if you have all of the basic information about what transpired and are trying to find a way to move forward.

6. Overt triggers and reminders. While it is normal for partners to deal with triggers and reminders, I have had several clients who can't let go and move on because they are facing overt triggers and reminders. Some examples of this would be seeing your partner's affair partner on a regular basis, keeping houses, cars, furniture, etc. that you know your partner used for their infidelity-related activities, taking care of a child that was the result of an affair, or knowing that your partner still works with their affair partner. If you are facing this type of situation, my first suggestion would be to remove the trigger (selling a house, car, etc.) or change the situation (you partner gets a new job). If this isn't possible, I recommend that you seek counseling or coaching to help you deal with the situation in a way that supports your recovery.

7. Attempting to control the wounding partner. Sometimes we as wounded partners fall into the trap of thinking that we can control our partner's behavior in an attempt to keep ourselves from future pain. The most common ways we might try to do this are through monitoring our partner's recovery, scrutinizing our partner's behavior on a daily (and even hourly) basis, and trying to control our partner's environment. While it's understandable why we might feel the need to do this, it can keep us so preoccupied with our partner's recovery that we fail to concentrate on our own. Additionally, if we don't let go of our control to see what our partner is going to do, we may end up wondering if they are only changing their behavior because we are making them do it. This can make it hard to let go and move on because it creates a feeling of insecurity.

8. Rumination. Rumination is most frequently associated with OCD, but we all do it to some extent. According to the OCD and Anxiety Center, rumination is defined as "engaging in a repetitive negative thought process that loops continuously in the mind without end or completion." While it is not easy to let thoughts of our partner's unfaithful actions go, a habit of rumination can greatly affect our mental health. Ruminating is common when people are facing ongoing stressors that they can't control and is often driven by a belief that, if we think about it long enough, we will gain some sort of insight that will solve our problems. Journaling can be greatly helpful when it comes to rumination. By jotting our thoughts down, we can begin to examine them in order to find potential solutions and/or put them in perspective. Meditation and therapy can also help with rumination.

9. PTSD. Immediately following the discovery of our partner's infidelity, most wounded partners will display PTSD-like symptoms. For the majority of us, these fade within 2-6 weeks of the discovery. However, it is not uncommon for a certain percentage of wounded partners to develop PTSD that needs to be treated. This is especially common if you have a history of trauma and/or have received multiple disclosures of details pertaining to your partner's infidelity-related behavior. The intrusive thoughts related to PTSD can create an anchor to the past that makes it difficult for us to let go of it. If you are having trouble letting go and suspect that PTSD might be an issue, I urge you to consult your doctor and/or a qualified therapist. Therapies such as Brainspotting, EMDR, IFS, Neurofeedback, and ETT have been proven to be helpful to those suffering from PTSD and other trauma-related issues.

1. Have you had trouble letting go of the past? If so, why do you think that is?

_____
_____
_____
_____

2. List some specific things that you are having trouble letting go of.

_____
_____
_____
_____

3. List at least two ways that letting go of these things might benefit you.

_____
_____
_____
_____

4. What were some of your dreams for the future prior to discovering your partner's infidelity?

_____
_____
_____
_____
_____

5. Do you see your dreams and goals for the future being within your control now? Why or why not?

_____
_____
_____
_____
_____

6. How could letting go of the past help you to dream for your future once more?

_____
_____
_____
_____
_____

CHAPTER 23

Life Beyond Betrayal

"The past is a place of reference, not a place of residence; the past is a place of learning, not a place of living." —Roy T. Bennett

The Road Ahead

I want to start off this section by stating that I know many of you reading this book will not be ready to think about moving on from your partner's infidelity at this time. Not only is this okay — it is completely normal. Recovering from the devastating effects of infidelity is a journey that can't be rushed. In my experience working with wounded partners, I have seen the bulk of recovery take place within 12-24 months, depending on the issues involved. My purpose in writing these remaining chapters is not to rush you or put you on a guilt trip for not moving fast enough. My wish is that you catch a glimpse of hope regarding what life could be like for you outside of the circumstances that are consuming you at this present time. While I have to be honest and tell you that your recovery will be an ongoing process, I will also tell you that it won't be the all-consuming task that you have experienced since you learned of your partner's behavior.

As I stated previously, recovery is a journey, and I want to give you a realistic view of what that journey might look like. The first year of recovery after the discovery or disclosure of infidelity is typically a challenging one. Holidays and anniversaries are particularly difficult during the first year. This can be intensified by "dribbling" disclosure because anniversaries aren't as clear and the first year can feel like one constant, non-stop anniversary.

There will be times, maybe even years down the road, when you will be reminded of the past and feel the familiar pain of betrayal. A favorite song, a certain season, or even a vacation are all things that can bring you back to that time in your life. I want you to know that this is normal. Just because you feel the pain once again doesn't mean that you haven't recovered or that you are moving backwards. Experiences like these are par for the course when it comes to infidelity recovery, so don't let them discourage you. Remember, betrayal is all about grieving losses and it is completely normal to feel those losses from time to time throughout your life.

Although I don't know your unique pain, I have experienced sexual betrayal in my previous marriage, and I do know at least a portion of what you are going through. I can tell you that, at first, I didn't know how I was ever going to have a good day again. The pain from my husband's betrayal seemed like it consumed every minute of every day for a very long time. However, as time passed, I found that I was able to go a whole day without thinking about it. Soon after that, I realized there were multiple days in a row that I didn't think about it, and it went on like that until I hardly ever thought about it at all. Now, over 26 years later, I have a completely new life and hardly ever think about those days gone by. Whether it's possible for you to stay in your current relationship, or you need to move on like I did, I want to encourage you that there can come a day when your pain is replaced with purpose, confidence, and happiness. You can smile once again.

1. Imagine your life in the future without the pain you are going through now. Write yourself a brief note about what you see for yourself outside of your current circumstances.

_____
_____
_____
_____
_____

Acceptance

"You can't stop the waves, but you can learn to surf."—Joseph Goldstein

If you remember from earlier in the book, I explained how acceptance was the final stage of the Kübler-Ross model of grief. I wrote that, while getting to acceptance can improve our outlook on the other stages of grief and on life in general, the idea that we're completely done is misleading. Acceptance doesn't mean that things are suddenly "all better". It means that we have now accepted our losses as part of our new reality and that we can stop trying to relive the past and now engage fully in our future. We understand that we can't change the past or regain what was lost, but that loss doesn't have to define our existence and there is plenty of potential for good things to happen moving forward.

This is what acceptance looks like during the initial phase of the grief cycle. However, I would like to expand on the idea of acceptance as you move past the first year. Although accepting what has happened as a part of our new reality is an important step in engaging in true recovery, I believe that our concept of acceptance can grow and expand as we move along our journey. Each one of us can discover a newfound state of acceptance as we gain new insights from our experiences. Here are four of the ways that I believe advanced acceptance plays itself out for those of us who have traveled past merely accepting events as they have happened:

1. We release ourselves from the victim role. We begin to see ourselves as survivors of infidelity instead of merely the victims of it. We start to recognize the inner strength that has been developed through adversity and we realize what new possibilities are open to us now that we have this strength. We understand that hanging onto a victim mentality tethers us to the past and prevents us from moving forward. We decide to take the reins of our own destiny and make empowered choices that will shape our future.

2. We learn from the past. Instead of running from the pain, we begin studying the past in order to learn from it. We are now strong enough to replay events in our mind in an attempt to look at those events through a new lens of knowledge and perspective. We see things in a different light and are able to learn from our mistakes as well as from our partner's behavior. We understand what the warning signs were and begin to formulate a plan on how to recognize them if they ever surface again, as well as what to do about it.

3. We release ourselves from the past. We acknowledge that, while we may wish we had done things differently, the past is in the past and no amount of wishing is going to change things. We forgive ourselves for our mistakes and forgive others for theirs. We are gentle with ourselves. We let go of regret in order to find peace.

4. We acknowledge that our partner's actions don't define us. We realize that our partner's actions have nothing to do with who we were then and nothing to do with who we are moving forward. We feel proud of who we are becoming and of our newfound strength and resolve. We understand that we deserve to be loved and to love freely. We acknowledge that, while the pain we have gone through is part of our story, it doesn't make up the entirety of it. We see that the future is wide open, with endless possibilities that we get to choose.

"We are infinitely more than our limitations or our afflictions."—Jeffrey R. Holland

1. Can you see yourself moving past the pain you are in now, and into acceptance? Why or why not? What would it look like if you were able to?

_____
_____
_____
_____

2. Besides the four ways listed above, can you think of any other ways that advanced acceptance could affect your life for the positive? If so, list them here.

_____
_____
_____
_____
_____

CHAPTER 24

Trusting Yourself Again

For many of us, one of the things that gets the most damaged when infidelity is discovered is trust in ourselves. How could we have chosen so poorly? How could we not have seen? Why did we stay so long? What if this happens again and we don't see it? These are just a few of the many questions that can haunt us as we try to move forward. For many of us, trusting ourselves after we have been betrayed is even more difficult than accepting what has happened.

After experiencing betrayal, it is common for us as wounded partners to have mixed feelings toward ourselves. We begin to doubt our own perception and ability to keep ourselves away from danger. This is especially true of wounded partners who experienced gaslighting as a feature of their relationship. (Gaslighting is a covert form of emotional abuse in which we are asked to accept a false narrative of events that contradict what we know to be reality.) Gaslighting is almost always present, at least to some extent, in relationships with intimacy avoidants (IAs), intimacy anorexics (IAs), and addicts. However, it can suddenly show up in relationships where these things are not present as well. Gaslighting frequently happens in standard relationships (those without addiction or IA present) when a wounded partner voices their suspicion and the unfaithful partner doesn't want to get caught. I work with many wounded partners who tell me that their partner acted like they were crazy for suspecting unfaithful behavior, only to find out later that their instincts were correct.

I have seen many wounded partners who have been in long-term relationships with IAs and addicts experience identity erosion. The term "identity erosion" describes a scenario in which someone involved in an unhealthy relationship loses sight of their hopes, dreams, opinions, and even the core of who they are. Identity erosion is present when we start taking on the opinions of others instead of holding true to our own beliefs about who we are. We are silenced into not voicing our objections and/or opinions for fear of upsetting our partner. Sometimes, we simply give up on our dreams and goals because they would interfere with the demands that are being placed on us. Many of my clients who are experiencing identity erosion have spent so much time being what the other person wanted them to be, they have forgotten who they used to be before the relationship. Life becomes very limited when this happens because self-trust is at the core of the decision-making process around trying new experiences in life. When we doubt our thoughts, abilities, and even the soundness of our own minds, it becomes difficult to accept new learning opportunities that might pull us outside of our comfort zone. The result is a stagnation in personal growth. This phenomenon is especially evident in those who have been in relationships with IAs and addicts because of the need for the addict or IA to justify their own behavior and not take any of the blame. Instead, the partner takes on more and more responsibilities, hoping their partner will give them the love they once had. The result is often a loss of identity.

Another feature of these types of relationships is what I refer to as "carrot dangling". This describes a scenario in which the wounding partner tells us that if we just do "x", we will get the love, honor, respect, etc. that we have been longing for. Unfortunately these things remain elusive because the person either moves the goalpost just before we arrive at it and/or gives us what we desire for a moment before deciding that we must jump through yet another hoop to keep it.

Whether continual betrayal defines your relationship, or your partner betrayed you only one time, the fact remains that regaining trust for ourselves is an obstacle that many of us will have to overcome if we are to truly heal. Many of us ask questions like, "how can I ever trust my partner again?" or, "how can I ever trust anyone again?" My answer to questions like these is that, after betrayal, we must first learn to trust ourselves again if we hope to ever trust anyone else. The reason for this is that we have to weigh the actions and words of others in order to determine whether or not we believe them. If we can't trust ourselves enough to interpret what we are seeing and hearing, we will tend to regard others with suspicion, regardless of whether they deserve that suspicion.

Here are some tips for rebuilding trust with yourself:

1. Commit to honest communication moving forward. When I explain to couples how to rebuild trust in their relationship, I always emphasize that the first step to rebuilding trust is honesty. The same holds true if we are to reestablish trust with ourselves. Honesty and transparency are crucial if you are ever to believe yourself again. This means committing to being brutally honest with yourself when it comes to your motives, beliefs, and behaviors. If you are excusing your partner's behavior, own up to that. If you are telling yourself that something isn't a big deal when it is, admit that to yourself. Self-delusion can have no place in your life if you are to trust yourself again.

2. Understand that it takes time. You didn't lose trust in yourself overnight, and you won't get it back overnight either. Don't put too much pressure on yourself to trust again. Instead, identify the steps you need to take and practice them over time.

3. Evaluate limiting beliefs. The task of trusting yourself may seem insurmountable, but it can be done. Instead of telling yourself it will be too hard, tell yourself that you have the ability to learn the right way to trust. Also check to see if you have any other limiting beliefs around yourself or your relationship that enable you to make excuses for your behavior or your partner's behavior.

4. Practice self-compassion. As you evaluate your motives, behavior, and beliefs, treat yourself with kindness. You may discover that some of the things driving your behavior are things you wish weren't a part of your life. Just remember that you are brave to look at them. Try to evaluate yourself objectively and refrain from judging yourself. Self-compassion is important during this process. You have already been hurt enough by your partner's actions. There is no need to hurt yourself further with self-judgement.

5. Establish safe routines. While you are learning to trust yourself again, it will be important for you to identify what actions you need to take on a regular basis in order to keep yourself safe. For example, you may need to take a timeout to evaluate your partner's words to determine whether or not they are gaslighting you. Or you may need to practice self-care in the form of good sleep hygiene or alone time to help ensure that your mind is at its sharpest. Whatever you decide is right for you, be sure to make these things non-negotiable.

6. Be consistent. As you practice your newfound way of being, try your best to remain consistent. This can be especially hard if we are in a relationship where our partner accuses us of being selfish or plays the victim. Hold your ground and get support where you need it. As you do this, you will find that your trust in yourself grows stronger every day.

1. Do you think that you are struggling with a lack of self-trust upon discovering your partner's infidelity? Why or why not?

_____
_____
_____
_____
_____

2. If you answered yes to Question #1, in what ways do you think that trust in yourself has been damaged by your partner's actions?

_____
_____
_____
_____
_____

As a side note, I want to mention that, for many of us, our upbringing plays a large part in our relationship decisions. It is not uncommon for wounded partners to tell me that they were gaslit by a parent or caregiver and, as a result, have never felt that they could trust themselves. The fact that they didn't trust themselves put them at a disadvantage and led many of them to stay in relationships with people who weren't trustworthy. For those of you struggling with this dynamic, I encourage you to begin to challenge the beliefs that you learned in childhood about your trustworthiness. You do have a sound mind. You can trust your instincts. Your thoughts, feelings, and beliefs are every bit as valid as anyone else's. Even though your upbringing can make trusting yourself all the more challenging, you can still learn to trust yourself, maybe even for the first time, using the steps outlined above.

I believe another key component to learning to trust ourselves again after betrayal lies in equipping ourselves with the knowledge it takes to recognize the signs that we are being mistreated or lied to.

Although each situation is different, here are some red flags to look for when you are trying to determine whether or not your partner is willing to change:

- Shows an unwillingness to be held accountable for their time or whereabouts.
- Shows an unwillingness to take a polygraph.
- Continues to gaslight you.
- Gives you the silent treatment when you ask them to be accountable.
- Denies, blames you, or acts like a victim when you bring up their bad behavior.
- Defends themselves in response to you sharing your feelings.
- Refuses to give you full access to their phone or computer.
- Continues to use alternate phones and computers that you don't have access to.

- Doesn't prioritize spending time with you over work and/or friends.

- Belittles you or minimizes your feelings.

- Disregards your requests for change, even though you've explained those requests multiple times.

Although these behaviors are undesirable and don't bode well for reconciliation, I do want to mention that many of them are present in the early stages of recovery. This will hold especially true for those of you in relationships with intimacy anorexics, intimacy avoidants, and those struggling with addiction. These behaviors are a sign of immaturity because the presence of addiction stunts emotional growth. If your partner exhibits any of these behaviors, my best advice would be for you to give them a limited amount of time to engage in recovery in order to see if they are willing to put in the effort necessary to change their behavior. If your partner is working hard at their recovery, and addiction or IA is the issue, you should begin to see some significant changes within 6 months. This amount of time should be sufficient to help you determine whether or not reconciliation is going to be a possibility. I also think it's important to add that I'm not advocating for these behaviors to be acceptable in any way. If you decide to stay for a certain amount of time to give reconciliation a chance, I recommend that you get the support that you need in order to help you draw and keep strong boundaries around your partner's behavior and help you understand instances where you might be making excuses for them.

If you are moving on from your current relationship, understanding what to look for in a potential partner is going to be crucial to trusting yourself in the future. Here are some of the most prevalent warning signs that you may not want to move forward with the relationship:

- They show a lack of empathy.

- They act entitled.

- They play the victim.

- They expect unwarranted praise.

- They have trouble regulating their emotions.
- They are defensive.
- They are sensitive to criticism and/or perceived criticism.
- They are often late or disrespect your time.
- They are aggressive.
- They exude a large amount of charm, charisma, and confidence.
- They have a history of cheating.
- They blame-shift.

- These are some of the most common signs of addicts, IAs, and/or people who are self-centered. If you see 2 or more of these signs, please be extra careful when deciding whether to move forward. It can be okay to give someone the benefit of the doubt, but if you have voiced your concerns more than once and they haven't made any changes to their behavior, you can safely assume that it's not your communication that is the issue. More likely than not, the person doesn't want to change. A self-centered person will want their way in relationships and won't seem to understand or respect the give and take that all good relationships need in order to stay healthy.

- Another method that can help you determine whether you want to stay in a new relationship or not is to pay close attention to a person's actions when they are under stress. Self-centered people tend to respond with anger and/or entitlement when things don't go their way. They are highly unlikely to adjust to the new situation and, when forced to do so, often do it begrudgingly. Conversely, a non-self-centered person may still feel stress, but will tend to respond with solutions and optimism about resolving the situation. Some important qualities to look for in a potential mate are they are someone who notices your needs on a regular basis and is *consistently* attentive to them, someone who meets you halfway, and someone who is willing to support you in your dreams and celebrates your successes, especially if your success doesn't benefit them directly.

The Role of Intuition

"The intuitive mind is a sacred gift, and the rational mind is a faithful servant. We have created a society that honors the servant and has forgotten the gift." – Albert Einstein

Intuition is a process that gives us the ability to know, or at least suspect, something without engaging in analytical reasoning. It can help bridge the gap between the conscious and unconscious parts of our mind. Scientists have not yet been able to pinpoint where exactly in the brain that intuition comes from, but many support a dual-process theory. This theory explains how thought is believed to arise in two different ways; both unconsciously and consciously. Intuition is theorized to come into conscious thought by way of the unconscious part of the mind. This is believed to happen when the unconscious mind processes hunches and matches them to past experiences and/or accumulated knowledge.

When it comes to betrayal, and relationships in general, intuition can be an important part of the decision-making process. It is important to understand that intuition can be faulty and, therefore, we shouldn't always depend on intuition alone. However, when combined with data or evidence, it is a powerful tool that we can use to our advantage. When we are repeatedly confronted with intuitive feelings that something just isn't right, we need to examine the source of those feelings in order to decide if we need to do something about them.

After betrayal, many of us struggling to trust ourselves again have misgivings about listening to our intuition. This is understandable and, in some cases, wise. Fear is a major issue that can override intuition and tell us things are wrong when they aren't. Here are some other obstacles we face that can block intuition:

1. Seeking approval from others
2. Overanalyzing the situation
3. Ego
4. Depression

5. Anxiety

6. Self-esteem

As you can see from the list above, many of the things that we experience as wounded partners can get in the way of our intuition. Even so, I advise that you start listening to it. Here is where it would be beneficial for you to enlist the help of a counselor or coach so that you can run your ideas and feelings by someone you trust to give you good advice, confirm your intuition, or let you know if you are heading in the wrong direction.

If you would like to work on developing your intuition, here are some tips:

1. Prioritize it. While it is important to understand that intuition is not fact, it is equally important to listen to yourself when you have a gut feeling about something. You can always check with a coach, counselor, mentor, or wise and trusted friend before acting on your intuition. However, ignoring it completely is a mistake. By prioritizing your intuition, you will soon begin to see where you are right and where you may need to work on things.

2. Learn where and how it shows up. For most people, intuition has a certain way of showing up. We've all heard the phrases "gut feeling" or "that smells off". For many people, intuition shows up in the five senses or in a particular area (like the gut) of the body. For others, it may show up in dreams, thought processes, or while engaging in creative activities. For some, intuition speaks directly and for others, indirectly.

3. Keep a journal. Sometimes, especially if we are out of practice, intuition shows up unbeknownst to us. Keeping a regular thought journal can be helpful when we are trying to develop our intuition, because we can revisit it to check for any recurring themes and/or patterns.

4. Practice mindfulness. People who practice mindfulness maintain an acute awareness throughout the day of thoughts, feelings, environment, and bodily sensations. A great way to practice mindfulness as it pertains to intuition is to do regular body scans to see if you can detect reactions that indicate that something is off. Another way to practice mindfulness is to acknowledge and accept your thoughts without judgement. For example, if something makes you angry, notice that you are angry without saying to yourself, "I wish I weren't angry" or, "I shouldn't be angry". Instead, recognize the presence of anger and decide if you need to do something about it or not.

When I work with clients who are learning to trust their intuition, I often ask them the following questions. These are questions that you could start asking yourself as you are learning to trust yourself again:

1. Does it seem/feel right to you?
2. Does that seem like the right answer?
3. What was your gut reaction to the situation?
4. What do you think the answer should be?
5. How did that situation make you feel?

In my experience, my clients tend to know what is best for them without me having to tell them unless they are being taken over with anger or fear. Quite often, my role as their coach is to guide them along the path to the truths they already hold inside. They begin to trust themselves again when, little by little, they test out their intuition and find that they are right most of the time. In the same way that our partner's actions, big and small, help us to decide whether or not we can trust them again, the practice of trusting our intuition and following through can be just the micro-trust we need to move toward fully trusting ourselves again or even for the very first time.

1. Are there any particular situations you are facing where you think you should pay attention to your intuition? If so, list them here.

_____
_____
_____
_____

2. List at least one person whom you can trust to give you good advice before acting on your intuition. Make a plan to talk to them about the scenario(s) you listed above.

_____
_____
_____
_____
_____

CHAPTER 25

Post-Traumatic Growth

I want to start off this chapter by saying that I initially debated whether or not to include it in this particular book. I was worried that some of you might read this section on post-traumatic growth as an attempt on my part to minimize the pain you are feeling from your current circumstances. It is not my intention to jump right into the possibility of growth as a way to callously bypass the impact of the real losses that you have suffered. I think it is important for you to understand that, if you are not ready to hear how your experience can be used for good, I completely understand. If this describes you, I suggest that you skip this section and come back at a later time. As I have stated a number of times throughout this book, recovery from infidelity cannot, and should not, be rushed. However, in the end, I decided to include this information because I know that some of you are ready to explore the subject of personal growth. I wanted to make sure you had this information in order to start to make sense out of the unnecessary suffering brought on by your partner's poor choices.

In the mid-1990's, two psychologists, Richard Tedeschi, PhD, and Lawrence Calhoun, PhD, developed a theory to explain why a number of survivors of traumatic events seem to grow from their experiences rather than becoming paralyzed by them. This theory, called post-traumatic growth theory (PTG theory), holds that people who experience psychological struggle, and even PTSD, after a traumatic event can eventually find personal growth through the time, effort, and struggle it takes them to overcome the pain caused by that event. (Tedeschi, et. al., 2006). Post-traumatic growth is often confused with resilience, but the two are not the same. While resiliency describes someone's capacity to recover quickly from difficulty, post-traumatic growth often happens despite a person's lack of resiliency. The ideas behind the theory of post-traumatic growth suggest that it is produced as a result of the struggle brought on by the lack of an ability to bounce back quickly. Someone who is naturally resilient won't experience post-traumatic growth because they are unlikely to be shaken to the core by their experience. The exciting thing about this theory is that it gives hope to those who have experienced even the most traumatic events. This is good news for us as wounded partners, as infidelity is one of the most traumatizing things a person can go through.

There are several signs that a person might exhibit if they are experiencing personal growth. These include:

1. A sense of personal strength. A newfound sense of personal strength can be gained when you take time to reflect on all of the obstacles you have had to overcome because of your experience with infidelity.

2. Improved relationships. This can happen in one of two ways. First, you may discover that you have people in your life who are willing to give you unconditional support and this strengthens your bond with them. Second, you may find that you are able to communicate your needs and boundaries more clearly within your relationships, which helps to strengthen them.

3. A new appreciation of life and love. One of the common outcomes that I have seen from trauma's impact on wounded partners is that they become more appreciative of the relationships they have in their lives.

4. An exploration of new possibilities. While the trauma of infidelity is not something that we would willingly invite into our lives, the fact that we have no choice in the matter can lead us to explore new possibilities. As Austrian psychiatrist Viktor Frankl once said, "When we are no longer able to change a situation, we are challenged to change ourselves."

5. Spiritual growth. When our deeply held beliefs are challenged, we often start asking the type of big questions that we might otherwise have overlooked in our daily lives. We can struggle to find answers to existential questions, and those answers can eventually lead to spiritual growth.

6. Increased compassion and altruism (the practice of selfless concern for the wellbeing of others). Many survivors of traumatic experiences develop a deep empathy and compassion for others who are facing similar situations. When we have suffered, we can choose to become bitter, or we can understand that our suffering can be a catalyst for helping others in need.

7. Creative growth. Although pain isn't the only catalyst for creativity, there is something to be said for the popular idea that great pain produces great art. Creativity can provide a powerful way for us to express and transform our feelings of pain.

According to Richard Tedeschi, PhD, one of the developers of PTG theory, a person is more likely to experience post-traumatic growth if they are open to reevaluating their experiences and if they are extroverted. (Collier, 2006). While we can't change whether we are an extrovert or an introvert, we do have some control over how open we are to new thoughts and ideas. Although studies suggest that post-traumatic growth often happens without coaching or psychotherapy, it can also be facilitated. (Tedeschi, 2020). Here are five ways that you can help yourself develop post-traumatic growth:

1. Understand that your beliefs are being challenged. When something traumatic happens, many of our core beliefs can be challenged. An example of how infidelity can do this is by challenging the sense of safety you had within your relationship. Infidelity can also challenge your sense of being enough, of worthiness, of belonging, of who your partner is, of who God is (if you believe in God), and even your sense of who you are. As a result, wounded partners often experience culture shock. Culture shock is defined as "the feeling of disorientation experienced by someone who is suddenly subjected to an unfamiliar culture, way of life, or set of attitudes". (Oxford Languages). Even though culture shock is often perceived as a negative event because of the negative feelings that accompany it, it can also present a unique opportunity for growth. This requires that we take the time to reflect on who we want to be and what our belief systems should be moving forward.

2. Learn to regulate your emotions. It will be hard for you to make the right decisions moving forward if your emotions are out of control. The reason for this, as explained at length in various sections of this book, is that the fight or flight response overrides our ability to think rationally. We need to manage the intense feelings brought on by the wounding partner's infidelity before we can hope to move forward in our recovery journey. Using the tools I mentioned in previous chapters such as somatic exercises, time-outs, anger work, self-care, trigger plans, and trigger mapping are all ways that can help you learn to regulate your emotions.

3. Talk about it. Talking about the trauma you've experienced from your partner's infidelity-related behavior is an important step in helping you process what has happened and decide how you want to respond. Sometimes hearing ourselves say something out loud is the catalyst we need to understand our situation. Enlisting the help of a coach or counselor who truly understands the onslaught of emotions brought on by infidelity will help you greatly during this time.

4. Rewrite your story. When you are ready, it is important for you to rewrite your story to include not only the traumatic event, but the success you have had so far in overcoming it. This is a chance for you to open your mind to new possibilities and learnings that could come from your experience. I invite you to move beyond your pain and into a world where you are not defined by your partner's infidelity.

5. Help others. One of the best ways to find meaning in unnecessary suffering is by helping others. Your experience will give a unique and much-needed perspective to someone who is enduring pain from infidelity. Additionally, your personal triumph over the trauma can give hope to someone who is in the middle of discovery or disclosure because they are likely wondering how they will ever make it through. Even a referral to one or more of the resources you have found helpful in your journey can be a lifeline to someone in pain.

6. List some of the ways your core beliefs have been challenged by your partner's infidelity.

_____
_____
_____
_____

7. Can you imagine sharing your story in order to help someone else? Why or why not?

_____
_____
_____
_____

8. Besides sharing your story, list other ways in which you could help someone with things you have learned through your experience with infidelity.

_____
_____
_____
_____

Parting Words

In closing, I would like to thank you for reading this book. I hope that it was helpful to you. While I know the road is long and tough to navigate, I encourage you to keep pressing on. As Winston Churchill once said, *"If you are going through hell, keep going."* If you do the work, don't give in, and seek help along the way, I know you will find your way out of the painful circumstances in which you have found yourself. I wish you healing, comfort, peace, and wholeness in your recovery journey.

References

American Psychiatric Association Website (2023), "Recovering Emotionally from Disaster", retrieved from https://www.apa.org/topics/disasters-response/recovering

Andreatta, B. (2017), "Wired to Resist", 7th Mind Publishing, Santa Barbara, CA

Armstrong, K. (2017), "I Feel Your Pain: The Neuroscience of Empathy", Association for Psychological Science, retrieved from https://www.psychologicalscience.org/observer/neuroscience-empathy

Arnsten, A., Raskind, M., Taylor, F., Connor, D. (2015), "The effects of stress exposure on prefrontal cortex: Translating basic research into successful treatments for post-traumatic stress disorder", Neurobiology of Stress, Vol. 1, p. 89-99, Bridges, A., Bergner, R., & Hesson-McInnis, M. (2003). Romantic partners' use of pornography: Its significance for women. Journal of Sex & Marital Therapy, 29(1), 1- 14.

Blair, RJ (2011), "Considering Anger from a Cognitive Neuroscience Perspective", WIREs Cognitive Science, 3(1), p. 65-74, https://doi.org/10.1002/wcs.154

Blease, C. (2014), "The Duty to be Well-Informed: The Case of Depression", Journal of Medical Ethics, 40(4), p. 225-229

Bower, S., Bower, G. (2004) *Asserting Yourself*, Da Capo Lifelong Books, Boston, MA

Boyes, A. (2018), "What is Psychological Shock? And 5 Tips for Coping",

Psychology Today, retrieved from https://www.psychologytoday.com/us/blog/in-practice/201803/what-is-psychological-shock-and-5-tips-coping

Bridges, W. (2004) *Transitions: Making Sense of Life's Changes*, Da Capo Lifelong Books, Boston, MA

Carroll, J. S., Busby, D. M., Willoughby, B. J., & Brown, C. C. (2017). The porn gap: Differences in men's and women's pornography patterns in couple relationships. *Journal of Couple & Relationship Therapy, 16*(2), 146–163. https://doi.org/10.1080/15332691.2016.1238796

Cedars-Sinai Staff (2019), "The Science of Kindness", Cedars Sinai, retrieved from https://www.cedars-sinai.org/blog/science-of-kindness.html

Cohen, H. Kaplan, Z., Matar, M., Loewenthal, U., Zohar, J., Richter-Levin, G. (2007), "Long-lasting behavioral effects of juvenile trauma in an animal model of PTSD associated with a failure of the autonomic nervous system to recover", European Neuropsychopharmacology, 17(6,7), p. 464-477, https://doi.org/10.1016/j.euroneuro.2006.11.003

Collier, L. (2016), "Growth After Trauma", Monitor on Psychology, 47(10), p. 48, retrieved from https://www.apa.org/monitor/2016/11/growth-trauma

Collins Dictionary Online, Shaming, retrieved from https://www.collinsdictionary.com/us/dictionary/english/shaming

De Martino, B., Camerer, C. F., and Adolphs, R. (2010). Amygdala damage eliminates monetary loss aversion. Proc. Natl. Acad. Sci. U.S.A. 107, 3788–3792. doi: 10.1073/pnas.0910230107

Devan, GS (1993), "Management of Grief", Singapore Medical Journal, Vol. 34, p. 445, retrieved from http://www.smj.org.sg/sites/default/files/3405/3405ia1.pdf

DeVille, D., Lee, S., (2012), "Brain Decoding: Opportunities and Challenges for Pattern Recognition", Pattern Recognition, 45(6), p. 2033-2034, https://doi.org/10.1016/j.patcog.2011.06.001

Dugas, D., Geosling, BJ, Shelton, J. (2019), "In Defense of Discomfort: The Role of Challenging Emotions in the Growth Toward Self-Authorship on a Weekend Retreat", Journal of College and Character, 20(1), p. 47-64, https://doi.org/10.1080/2194587X.2018.1559200

Freyd, J. (1997), "Violations of Power, Adaptive Blindness and Betrayal Trauma Theory", Feminism and Psychology, 7(1), https://doi.org/10.1177/0959353597071004

Freyd, J., Deprince, A., Gleaves, D. (2007), "The state of betrayal trauma theory: Reply to McNally—Conceptual issues, and future directions", Memory, Vol. 15, Issue 3, https://doi.org/10.1080/09658210701256514

Hilton, Donald L. (2013) "Pornography addition-a supranormal stimulus considered in the context of neuroplasticity", Socioaffective Neuroscience & Psychology, 3:1, DOI: 10.3402/snp.v3i0.20767

Fisher, P. (2012) "Clinical Psychology: An Information Processing Approach", Encyclopedia of Human Behavior, p. 510-516, https://doi.org/10.1016/B978-0-12-375000-6.00205-6

Fotiadis, A., Abdulrahman, K., Spyridou, A. (2019), "The Mediating Roles of Psychological Autonomy, Competence and Relatedness on Work-Life Balance and Well-Being", Frontiers in Psychology, Vol. 10, https://doi.org/10.3389/fpsyg.2019.01267

Frey, E.D., Epkins, C.C. (2002), "Examining cognitive models of externalising and internalising problems in subgroups of juvenile delinquents. *Journal of Clinical Child and Adolescent Psychology*, 31 (4), 556-566.

Grossman, P., Neimann, L., Schmidt, S., Walach, H. (2004), "Mindfulness-based stress reduction and health benefits: A meta-analysis", Journal of Psychosomatic Research, 57(1), p. 35-43, https://doi.org/10.1016/S0022-3999(03)00573-7

Harris, R. (2019) *ACT made simple: an easy-to-read primer on acceptance and commitment therapy* (2nd ed.). New Harbinger Publications.

Harvard Medical School Online (2020), "Understanding the Stress Response", retrieved from https://www.health.harvard.edu/staying-healthy/understanding-the-stress-response

Hendricks, L., Bore, S., Aslinia, D., Morriss, G. (2013) "The Effects of Anger on the Brain and Body", National Forum Journal of Counseling and Addiction, 2(1), retrieved from http://www.nationalforum.com/Electronic%20Journal%20Volumes/Hendricks,%20LaVelle%20The%20Effects%20of%20Anger%20on%20the%20Brain%20and%20Body%20NFJCA%20V2%20N1%202013.pdf

Iniguez, G., Govezensky, T., Dunbar, R., Kaski, K. Barrio, R. (2014). "Effects of deception in social networks", Proceedings of the Royal Society B Biological Sciences, 281(1790), https://doi.org/10.1098/rspb.2014.1195

Kaufmann, T., Elvsåshagen, T., Alnæs, D., Zak, N., Pedersen, B., Norbom, L., Quraishi, S., Tagliazucchi, E., Laufs, H., Bjørnerud, A., Malt, U., Andreassen, O., Evangelos, R., Duff, E., Smith, S., Groote, I., Westlye, L. (2016), "The brain functional connectome is robustly altered by lack of sleep", NeuroImage, Vol. 127, p. 324-332, https://doi.org/10.1016/j.neuroimage.2015.12.028

Kim, EJ, Kim, JJ, Pellman, B. (2015) "Stress Effects on the Hippocampus: A Critical Review", Learning & Memory, 22(9), p. 411-416

Kimble, M., Sripad, A., Sobelewski, S., Fleming, K. (2018), "Negative world views after trauma: Neurophysiological evidence for negative expectancies", Psychological Trauma: Theory, Research, Practice, and Policy, *10*(5), 576–584. https://doi.org/10.1037/tra0000324

Koenigs, M., Grafman, J. (2009), "Posttraumatic Stress Disorder: The Role of Medial Prefrontal Cortex and Amygdala", The Neuroscientist, 15(5), https://doi.org/10.1177/1073858409333072

Koulouris, S., Pastromas, S., Sakellariou, D., Kratimenos, T., Piperopoulos, P., Manoli, A. (2010), "Takotsubo Cardiomyopathy: The "Broken Heart Syndrome", Hellenic J Cardiol, 51(5), 451-7

Lambert, N., Negash, S., Stillman, T., Olmstead, S., Fincham, F. (2012), "A Love That Doesn't Last: Pornography Consumption and Weakened Commitment to One's Romantic Partner", Journal of Social & Clinical Psychology, https://doi.org/10.1521/jscp.2012.31.4.410

Lancer, D. (2018) "How Secrets and Lies Destroy Relationships", Psychology Today, retrieved from https://www.psychologytoday.com/us/blog/toxic-relationships/201801/how-secrets-and-lies-destroy-relationships

Leotti LA, Iyengar SS, Ochsner KN. Born to choose: the origins and value of the need for control. Trends Cogn Sci. 2010 Oct;14(10):457-63. doi: 10.1016/j.tics.2010.08.001. PMID: 20817592; PMCID: PMC2944661.

Lester, T. (2021), "Emotional Maturity in Relationships", Psychology Today, retrieved from https://www.psychologytoday.com/us/blog/staying-sane-inside-insanity/202110/emotional-maturity-in-relationships

Levine, LJ (1997), "Reconstructing Memory for Emotions", Journal of Experimental Psychology, 126(2), p, 165-177, https://psycnet.apa.org/doi/10.1037/0096-3445.126.2.165

Mayo Clinic, n.d., "Complicated Grief", retrieved from https://www.mayoclinic.org/diseases-conditions/complicated-grief/symptoms-causes/syc-20360374#:~:text=Anxiety%2C%20including%20PTSD,living%2C%20relationships%20or%20work%20activities

Maercker, A., Neimeyer, R. A., Simiola, V. (2017). Depression and complicated grief. In S. N. Gold (Ed.), APA handbook of trauma psychology: Foundations in knowledge (pp. 185–194). American Psychological Association. https://doi.org/10.1037/0000019-011

Munhall, P. (1993), "Women's Anger and Its Meanings: A Phenomenological Perspective", Health Care for Women International, 14(6), p. 481-491, https://doi.org/10.1080/07399339309516078

Neff, K. (2015) *Self Compassion: The Proven Power of Being Kind to Yourself*, HaperCollins Publishers, New York, NY

NIH Library (2014), "Understanding the Impact of Trauma", Trauma-Informed Care in Behavioral Health Services, TIP Series, No. 57, retrieved from https://www.ncbi.nlm.nih.gov/books/NBK207191/

Oxford Languages, Boundary, retrieved from https://www.oxfordlearnersdictionaries.com/us/definition/english/boundary#:~:text=%2F%CB%88ba%CA%8Andri%2F-,%2F%CB%88ba%CA%8Andri%2F,or%20places%3B%20a%20dividing%20line

Raghunathan, R. (2016), "Why Losing Control Can Make You Happier", Greater Good Magazine, Berkeley, retrieved from https://greatergood.berkeley.edu/article/item/why_losing_control_make_you_happier#:~:text=Can%20seeking%20control%20undermine%20happiness,control%20can%20make%20you%20miserable.

Rasmussen, K. (2016), "A Historical and Empirical Review of Pornography and Romantic Relationships: Implications for Family Researchers", Journal of Family Theory and Review, https://doi.org/10.1111/jftr.12141

Real, Terrence (2018) *Fierce Intimacy: Standing Up to One Another with Love*, Sounds True, Audio Book Only

Smith, J. (2009), "What Happens When Compassion Hurts?", Greater Good Magazine, retrieved from https://greatergood.berkeley.edu/article/item/what_happens_when_compassion_hurts

Stanford University, Faculty Staff Help Center, retrieved from https://helpcenter.stanford.edu/resources/work-related-resources/coping-traumatic-stress

Stuewig, J., Tangney, J., Heigel, C., Harty, L., McCloskey, L. (2010), "Shaming, Blaming, and Maiming: Functional Links Among the Moral Emotions, Externalization of Blame, and Aggression", J Res Pers. 2010 Feb 1;44(1):91-102. doi: 10.1016/j.jrp.2009.12.005. PMID: 20369025; PMCID: PMC2848360

Tedeschi, R. (2020), "Growth After Trauma", Harvard Business Review, retrieved from https://hbr.org/2020/07/growth-after-trauma#:~:text=Although%20posttraumatic%20growth%20often%20happens,%2C%20narrative%20development%2C%20and%20service.

Tedeschi, R., Shakespeare-Finch, J., Taku, K., Calhoun, L. (2006) *Posttraumatic Growth: Theory, Research, and Applications First Edition*, Routledge Media Company, Oxfordshire, England, UK

Weiss, D. (2010), *Intimacy Anorexia: Healing the Hidden Addiction in Your Marriage*, Discovery Press

Woolley, K., Fishbach, A. (2022), "Motivating Personal Growth by Seeking Discomfort", Psychological Science, 33(4), https://doi.org/10.1177/09567976211044685

Worden, W. (1991), *Grief Counseling and Grief Therapy: A Handbook for the Mental Health Practitioner*, Routledge Media Company, Oxfordshire, England, UK

Yadav, PK, Yadav, RL, Sapkota, NK (2017) "Anger; It's Impact on the Human Body", Innovare Journal of Health Sciences, 4(5), 3-5

Zitzman, S., Butler, M. (2009) — "Wives' Experience of Husbands' Pornography Use and Concomitant Deception as an Attachment Threat in the Adult Pair-Bond Relationship", Sexual Addiction and Compulsivity: The Journal of Treatment & Prevention.

www.ingramcontent.com/pod-product-compliance
Lightning Source LLC
LaVergne TN
LVHW081455060526
838201LV00051BA/1803